THE

ANTIQUES MARKET BROWSERS' MARKS GUIDE

TO

SILVER

POTTERY AND PORCELAIN

EARTHENWARE

OLD SHEFFIELD PLATE

ELECTROPLATE

D1044317

THE

ANTIQUES MARKET BROWSERS' MARKS GUIDE

TO

SILVER

POTTERY AND PORCELAIN

EARTHENWARE

OLD SHEFFIELD PLATE

ELECTROPLATE

foulsham
LONDON • NEW YORK • TORONTO • SYDNEY

foulsham

The Publishing House, Bennetts Close,
Cippenham, Slough, Berks SL1 5AP

ISBN: 0–572–02341–3

Printed in Great Britain by Cox & Wyman Ltd., Reading.

Contents

Introduction

With the increased interest in antiques fairs and boot fairs, more and more people are becoming collectors of interesting pieces of silverware, porcelain or pottery. And once they are hooked on collecting, it follows that they want to know more about the items they admire and have bought for their home.

This handy guide is designed to help you to identify pieces of silver and silver plate, pottery and porcelain so that you can find out more about them, or have a better idea of their value. Conveniently arranged so that the actual mark on the piece is your first point of reference, you can then find out its date and details of the maker. Simple to use and full of useful information, it will be invaluable in your trips to antique shops and markets.

If you want to move on to more detailed information, you can find it in other books by Foulsham:

English Silver Hallmarks (0–572–01181–4)

English Pottery and Porcelain Marks (0–572–00711–6)

The Identification and Dating of Sheffield Electroplated Wares 1843–1943 (0–572–02310–3)

Silver

Both silver and gold have been much sought after for their beauty and usefulness since ancient times, and both, particularly gold, are quite rare. The value resulting from these properties has always proved a temptation to forgers and so marks were developed to prove which items were the real thing. In order to fully understand the significance of these marks it is important to know a little of the background. This will make your browsing far more interesting, and it will ensure that you don't overlook a really valuable piece! Keep the tables with you and you will be able to identify exactly what you have before you.

Silver hall-marks

Hall-marks are the authenticating marks struck on all modern and most old English, Scottish and Irish silver and gold. Strictly speaking they are the official marks confirming that the standard, or quality, of the metal is correct. More loosely the term is also used to describe the marks which show where an item was made or tested for purity, who made it and its date.

Hall-marking dates from 1300 A.D. when it was declared that no piece of silver 'was to depart out of the hands of the workers' until it had been assayed (or tested) and marked with the leopard's head. The standard was to be 92.5 per cent pure silver, the same as for coinage.

The *leopard's head*, which was crowned until 1821, was originally a standard mark. However, when the lion passant gardant was introduced as a hall-mark in 1544, it became more accurately the authoritative mark of the Goldsmiths' Company. As such, it was used by several provincial assay offices in addition to their own town mark. These were York and Newcastle, until those offices closed in 1857 and 1883 respectively; Chester until 1838 and Exeter until 1777. It has also been found on some Bristol silver from about 1720–1760.

The *lion passant gardant* first appeared in 1544 when

Henry VIII debased the coinage to only one third silver and so the new mark was struck, perhaps by the Goldsmiths' Company, to indicate that their hall-marked wares were sterling. In 1720, when the sterling standard was reintroduced (see below, Britannia Standard) use of the mark was extended to all the existing provincial English assay offices, and it was adopted in both Sheffield and Birmingham when they opened in 1773. In Chester, York and Sheffield, the lion remained *gardant*, that is, looking over its shoulder, but in London it changed to being merely *passant* (looking ahead) in 1821, in Exeter in 1837, in Newcastle in 1846 and in Birmingham in 1875.

The *Britannia Standard* was introduced in 1696 to put an end to the melting and clipping of coinage by silversmiths who had been using coins as cheap 'raw material'. The new standard for silver ware was 95.8 per cent pure silver, higher than the 92.5 per cent required for coinage. New hall-marks were ordered, 'the figure of a woman commonly called Britannia' replaced the lion passant and leopard's head crowned as the standard mark, and the lion's head erased (torn off at the neck) replaced the leopard's head crowned as the mark of origin.

Since the Britannia standard silver was more expensive, some silversmiths began to clamour for the restoration of sterling. Others preferred the new higher standard because the silver was softer and therefore easier to work with, and it sold well abroad. In 1720 the old sterling standard was restored but permission was given to retain the higher Britannia standard alongside it.

Since the 1973 Hall-marking Act came into force in January 1975 the English assay offices – London, Birmingham and Sheffield – have used the lion passant on sterling silver, while Edinburgh has used the lion rampant. All four assay offices use the Britannia mark on silver of the higher quality Britannia standard.

standard mark

The Maker's Mark

In order to ensure that standards were enforced it clearly was necessary for the authorities to be able to identify any makers of substandard wares, so in 1363 it was decreed that each Master Goldsmith should have his own mark and each mark had to be registered. The earliest marks were mainly symbols, but later makers often incorporated initials as well, or used initials on their own. In 1696, when a new higher British Standard was introduced, all makers had to re-register their marks and all had to include the first two letters of their surname. This rule lasted until 1720 when the old sterling standard was restored and, along with it, the old style makers' marks. For a few years there was some overlap, with some makers using marks of the different types at the same time, so in 1739 all were ordered to re-register with new marks. From that date onwards most marks consisted of initials of forename and surname, with only the occasional additional symbol such as a crown or a mullet.

maker's mark

The Date Letter

Towards the end of the fifteenth century continued complaints about substandard wares led to a ruling that the Assay Master should be responsible for maintaining the standard. This rule probably itself resulted in the date letter system, which was designed to make it possible to trace an offending Assay Master – just as the makers' mark made it possible to trace dishonest makers. The first full cycle of date letters in London started with A in 1478. The letters J and V to Z were omitted and the resulting 20 year cycles continued without a break until 1696, each being distinguished by a different style of lettering. Following London's lead, other assay offices adopted their own date lettering marks, including Edinburgh in 1681 and Dublin in 1638.

Until 1974, establishing the exact date of an item was complicated by the fact that the lengths of each cycle and the year of commencement varied from one assay office to another. Furthermore, each assay office changed its date letter at a different time of year. In 1975 all the remaining operational assay offices (London, Birmingham, Sheffield and Edinburgh) adopted the same lettering cycle and agreed to change the date letter on January 1st. In 1986 the Dublin Assay Office followed suit and started a new cycle, at A, on January 1st.

The Duty Mark

In 1720 a duty of 6d. an ounce was levied on wrought plate. Some silversmiths dodged paying this duty, which was levied at the time of assay, by incorporating pieces of plate bearing hall-marks into new items. The duty was removed in 1758 but reimposed in 1784, when a new, additional, hall-mark was introduced – the sovereign's head mark – specifically to prove that duty had been paid. From December 1784 until May 1786 the king's head was incuse, but from then until the duty was abolished in 1890 the head appeared in cameo. The profiles of George III, George IV and William IV face to the right, that of Queen Victoria to the left. Besides the English assay offices, the duty mark was struck in Edinburgh, Glasgow and Dublin. Not every assay office bothered to change the head on the death of the monarch, and the profile of William IV sometimes appears on Victorian silver made as late as 1841.

duty mark

Assay Offices outside London

Research into historical documents has revealed that there were once dozens of provincial centres producing marked silver items, from Barnstaple in the south west to Leeds in the north. However, only a few survived as assay towns into the 18th or 19th centuries, namely Chester, Norwich, Newcastle, Exeter, York and Bristol. York and Norwich declined as manufacturing centres for the trade during the 17th century and were almost dormant by 1700, but Exeter, Newcastle and Chester continued to be active throughout the 18th century, using as their town marks a triple castle, three keeps and the Arms of the City of Chester respectively.

By the middle of the 18th century, both Birmingham and Sheffield were fast becoming large manufacturing centres for the silver trade. In 1773, despite opposition from the London Goldsmith's Company, an Act of Parliament set up the Birmingham and Sheffield Assay Offices. Birmingham took an anchor as its mark and Sheffield a crown. When the Hall-marking Act came into force in 1975, the Sheffield Assay Office adopted a York rose as its mark in place of the crown.

Scotland

Scotland was not subject to the Britannia Standard, but in 1720, when sterling was restored in England, the standard of silver in Scotland was raised to conform with it, and the same 6d. an ounce duty was imposed.

From as far back as the 15th century Edinburgh silver was stamped with a maker's mark, a town mark – then as now the triple towered castle – and a Deacon's (or Warden's) mark. In 1681 a date letter system was introduced, and at the same time an Assay Master's mark was substituted for that of the Deacon. In 1759 the Assay Master's mark was replaced by the thistle standard mark.

Glasgow had an incorporation of Hammermen as early as 1536, and a date letter system was adopted in 1681, though it fell into disuse in the 18th century. An official Assay Office was set up in 1819 and the lion rampant was chosen as the standard mark. The sovereign's head duty mark was also struck, and in 1914 the thistle standard mark was added. The Glasgow Assay Office closed in 1964.

Until the rise of Glasgow, Aberdeen was probably the most important trading centre in Scotland outside Edinburgh. From about 1600 onwards various marks were used by the silversmiths, usually in the form of the letters AB, ABD or a contracted symbol, with a single or three castle mark.

Silver was made in Banff from about 1680 to 1830. Various versions of the name, from B to BANF were struck.

Silver made in Dundee was stamped with a pot of lilies from about 1625 to 1810, a device based on the town arms.

Various marks were used in Perth, including the lion and banner of St. John and, from the 18th century until about 1850, a double headed eagle (the modern town symbol).

Silversmiths worked in Inverness from about 1640 to 1880, and besides the more usual INS abbreviation a dromedary mark was sometimes used.

Montrose stamped a rose mark on silver from about 1650 to 1820, and Greenock a 'green oak' from about 1760 to 1840. At Wick and Tain the brief names were usually struck in full, while Elgin was contracted to Eln or Elg and used with a mother and child device.

Ireland

The Irish silversmiths undoubtedly have the longest unbroken history of any in the British Isles, dating back to the Bronze Age craftsmen. The Dublin goldsmiths were granted a charter in 1555, which was followed by a Royal Charter in 1637. This prescribed the sterling standard, with the harp crowned as the standard mark. In 1638 a date letter system began but it was only haphazardly used. In 1730 a duty of 6d. an ounce was imposed and the duty paid indicated by a figure of Hibernia. From 1806 Irish silver was struck with the king's head duty mark as well, so that the Hibernia tended to become the Dublin Assay Office mark.

Although the Dublin Assay Office has always been the only one in Ireland, there were guilds in several provincial cities. Silversmiths in Cork stamped their wares with a castle, sometimes accompanied by a ship, until the early 18th century, after which most seem to have used their own name punch and the word Sterling or Starling. A castle mark was also used in Limerick from about 1660 to 1710 when again some form of the word Sterling took over.

The Use and Abuse of Hall-marks

Invaluable though hall-marks are to the silver collector as a guide to quality, date, provenance and maker, they can be misleading if they are totally relied on without any reference to the piece on which they appear. They can even lay the unwary collector open to wiles of forgers.

Always take care when looking at the shapes of shields or outlines of the punch, the style of the town mark, standard mark or date letter and the actual appearance and crispness of the marks as well as their position on the piece. Hall-marks are struck with very carefully made dies which leave a sharp impression even after long years of use. A 'soft' mark is one of the signs of a faker who has not the time nor money to make high grade dies. Of course, marks can become 'rubbed' over time, but one should certainly be suspicious of a fairly good Britannia mark alongside a very rubbed maker's mark and date letter. On the other hand, very few makers' marks are quite as crisply struck as the official hall-marks.

The placing of marks is also important. For example, a London-made tankard and cover from the 17th century would be marked to the right of the handle, near the rim, and across the cover, whereas a mid-18th century one would be marked on the base. Until 1780, spoons and forks were marked near the bowl end, after that they were marked near the end of the stem.

Remember that not all good antique silver bears full hall-marks. Assay offices sometimes made mistakes, omitting, say, the date letter and striking the lion passant twice. Further, pieces made to special order were not always sent for assay, because the law only applied to pieces 'set for sale'.

Besides being misled as to date, maker or provenance, it is possible to mistake whether a particular item is silver at all. The status of the hall-mark led to many imitations, first among pewterers and later by the makers of plated goods. Many marks on Old Sheffield Plate and close-plated wares and, from around 1860, on electro-plated wares, look quite like silver marks. The degree of imitation on Sheffield Plate led to restrictions such that from 1784 most Sheffield Plate marks include the maker's full name. Electroplated wares sometimes carry marks which resemble silver hall-marks, but you will usually also find the letters EP, EPNS (on nickel plate) or EPBM (on Britannia metal). On items that have seen much use it is also often possible to detect the base metal core.

The Hall-marking Act

The reasons for hall-marking is to protect purchasers against fraud. There have been various pieces of legislation over hundreds of years designed to achieve this result. Today hall-marking is governed by the Hall-marking Act of 1973, which has simplified them and made them easier to understand. The Act came into force on January 1st 1975 and governs the hall-marking of silver, gold and platinum at the four UK assay offices – London, Birmingham, Sheffield and Edinburgh. The main points to note are:

• hall-marks must now consist of a maker's (or sponsor's) mark, the Standard Mark, the Assay Mark and the Date Letter. (Edinburgh uses the lion rampart for sterling silver.)
• all silver items weighing more than 7.8g must be hall-marked (1g for gold, 0.5g for platinum).

THE MARKS ON GOLD

Until 1798 the marks used on gold were the same as those for silver. From that date on, both 18 ct. and 22 ct. gold were permitted and were to be indicated by the relevant figures (.916 for 22 ct. and .750 for 18 ct. gold) and by a crown, which replaced the lion passant standard mark.

In 1854 three lower standards were introduced, which were indicated by the carat number plus the value in decimals: 9 with .375, 12 with .5, 15 with .625. The crown mark was reserved for 18 ct. and 22 ct. standards.

In 1931 12 ct. and 15 ct. were replaced by 14 ct. (.585).

In Sheffield, which has been licensed to assay goldwares since 1903, the gold mark is a rose. Edinburgh uses the thistle on 18 ct. and 22 ct. gold instead of the crown. In Glasgow, until its closure in 1964, the Lion Rampant appeared on all permitted standards.

In Ireland, from 1784, there have been three standards for gold – 22 ct. marked with the figures and the crowned harp and Hibernia; 20 ct marked with the figures and a plume of feathers; 18 ct. marked with the figures and a unicorn's head.

makers' mark   assay mark   standard mark   date letter

GOLD MARKS

GOLD STANDARD MARKS
British   **Imported**   **ASSAY OFFICES**
                                British   **Imported**

22 carat   22 carat   London

18 carat   18 carat   Birmingham

14 carat   14 carat   Sheffield

9 carat   9 carat   Edinburgh

GOLD MARKS

IRISH STANDARD MARKS	IRISH IMPORTED

22 carat

22 carat

20 carat

18 carat

18 carat

14 carat

14 carat

9 carat

9 carat

The Marks on Platinum

Since the introduction of legislation following the 1973 Hall-marking Act all articles containing platinum at 950 parts per 1000 or more must be hall-marked. Alloys below this standard may not be described as platinum.

The first year for marking platinum as 1975, starting with the letter 'A'.

makers' mark

platinum mark

assay mark

date letter

PLATINUM MARKS

STANDARD MARKS		ASSAY OFFICES	
British	Imported	British	Imported

London

Birmingham

Sheffield

INTRODUCTION TO THE TABLES

The aim of the Tables on the following pages is to enable you to discover much more about the pieces of silver that you come across.

The first set of Tables (p.17–70) show the Assay Office Marks of London, Birmingham, Chester, Dublin, Edinburgh, Exeter, Glasgow, Newcastle, Norwich, Sheffield and York. You will notice that each date letter cycle is contained in a separate box. At the outside edge of each box is a panel containing enlarged illustrations of the relevant Assay Office symbol and a sample date letter in the style of the boxed cycle. This should help you to find where to look for the actual mark you want just by flipping through the pages. The side panels of each box also contains details of the monarchs reigning at the time.

The second set of Tables (p.71–121) contains a large selection of Makers' Marks from 1697 to 1900. Most of them belong to London silver-smiths, but the most important makers from Birmingham, Dublin, Edinburgh and Sheffield have also been included.

Our reference source has been the official records held by the Goldsmith's Company in London, whose permission and kind assistance we had in being allowed to photograph the marks. It should be noted that while every individual entry is accurate they are not proportionally accurate to one another since all have been enlarged to a size appropriate to these pages, whatever their original size.

1544	G			
1545	H			Henry VIII 1547 Edward VI 1553 Mary
1546	I			
1547	K			G
1548	L			
1549	M			
1550	N			
1551	O			
1552	P			
1553	Q			
1554	R			
1555	S			
1556	T			
1557	V			

Eliz. I			1564		1572	
	1558		1565		1573	
	1559		1566		1574	
	1560		1567		1575	
	1561		1568		1576	
			1569		1577	
	1562		1570			
	1563		1571			

Eliz. I	1578		1585	H		
	1579	A	1586	I J	1592	P
	1580	B	1587	K	1593	Q
	181	C	1588	L	1594	R
	1582	D	1589	M	1595	S
	1583	E	1590	N	1596	T
	1584	F	1591	O	1597	V
		G				

Eliz. I	1598		1605		1613	Q
1603 James I	1599	A	1606	I J	1614	R
	1600	B	1607	K	1615	S
	1601	C	1608	L	1616	T
	1602	D	1609	M	1617	V
	1603	E	1610	O		
	1604	F	1611	O		
		G	1612	P		

		Year		Year		Monarch
		1625	🛡	1633	q	
1618	a	1626	i	1634	r	James I
1619	b	1627	k	1635	s	1625
1620	c	1628	l	1636	t	Charles I
1621	d	1629	m	1637	v	
1622	e	1630	n			
1623	f	1631	o			
1624	g	1632	p			

		Year		Year		Monarch
		1645	B	1652	P	
1638	a	1646	I	1653	Q	Charles I
1639	B			1654	R	1649
1640	C	1647	B	1655	S	Charles II
1641	D	1648	T	1656	T	
1642	E	1649	V	1657	B	
1643	ff	1650	R			
1644	O	1651	O			

		Year		Year		Monarch
		1665	H	1672	P P	
1658	A	1666	I	1673	Q	
1659	B	1667	K	1674	R	Charles II
1660	C			1675	S	
1661	D	1668	L	1676	T	
1662	E	1669	M	1677	V	
1663	F	1670	N			
1664	G	1671	O			

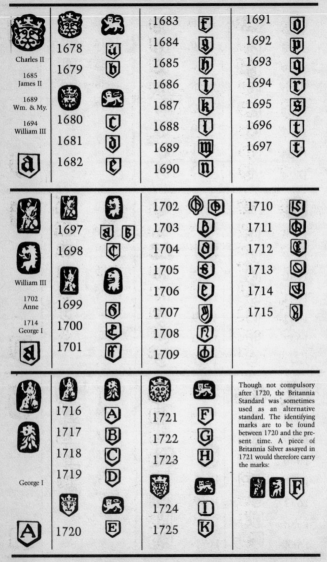

Charles II

1685
James II

1689
Wm. & My.

1694
William III

1678

1679

1680

1681

1682

1683

1684

1685

1686

1687

1688

1689

1690

1691

1692

1693

1694

1695

1696

1697

William III

1702
Anne

1714
George I

1697

1698

1699

1700

1701

1702

1703

1704

1705

1706

1707

1708

1709

1710

1711

1712

1713

1714

1715

George I

1716

1717

1718

1719

1720

1721

1722

1723

1724

1725

Though not compulsory after 1720, the Britannia Standard was sometimes used as an alternative standard. The identifying marks are to be found between 1720 and the present time. A piece of Britannia Silver assayed in 1721 would therefore carry the marks:

20

		1732	R			
1726	L	1733	S	Between 1719 and 1729 one should expect to find numerous variations of the Leopard's Head and Lion Passant marks.		
1727	M	1734	T			
1728	N	1735	V			
1729	O					
1730	P	Between 1716 and 1728 one should expect to find an occasional variation of the shield shape:				
1731	Q					L

		1742	g	1750	P	George II
1736	a	1743	h			
1737	b	1744	i	1751	q	
1738	c	1745	k	1752	r	
1739	d	1746	l	1753	s	
1740	e e	1747	m	1754	t	
1741	f	1748	n	1755	u	a
		1749	o			

		1763	H	1771	Q	George II
1756	A	1764	I	1772	R	1760 George III
1757	B	1765	K	1773	S	
1758	C	1766	L	1774	T	
1759	D	1767	M	1775	U	
1760	E	1768	N			
1761	F	1769	O			A
1762	G	1770	P			

George III	1776	**a**	1783	**h**	1791	**q**
	1777	**b**	1784	**i**	1792	**r**
	1778	**c**	1785	**k**	1793	**s**
	1779	**d**	1786	**l**	1794	**t**
	1780	**e**	1787	**m**	1795	**u**
	1781	**f**	1788	**n**		
a	1782	**g**	1789	**o**	An alternative shield may be found:
			1790	**p**		

George III	1796	**A**	1803	**H**	1811	**Q**
	1797	**B**	1804	**I**	1812	**R**
	1798	**C**	1805	**K**	1813	**S**
	1799	**D**	1806	**L**	1814	**T**
	1800	**E**	1807	**M**	1815	**U**
	1801	**F**	1808	**N**		
A	1802	**G**	1809	**O**	An alternative shield may be found:
			1810	**P**		

George III	1816	**a**	1821	**f**	1828	**n**
1820 George IV	1817	**b**	1822	**g**	1829	**o**
1830 William IV	1818	**c**	1823	**h**	1830	**p**
	1819	**d**	1824	**i**	1831	**q**
	1820	**e**	1825	**k**	1832	**r**
			1826	**l**	1833	**s**
a			1827	**m**	1834	**t**
					1835	**u**

1836	1843	1851	William IV
1836	1843	1851	
1837	1844	1852	William IV
1838	1845	1853	1837
1839	1846	1854	Victoria
1840	1847	1855	
1841	1848		
1842	1849	An alternative shield may be found:	
	1850		

1856	1863	1871	Victoria
1856	1863	1871	
1857	1864	1872	Victoria
1858	1865	1873	
1859	1866	1874	
1860	1867	1875	
1861	1868		
1862	1869	An alternative shield may be found:	
	1870		

1876	1883	1891	Victoria
1876	1883	1891	
1877	1884	1892	Victoria
1878	1885	1893	
1879	1886	1894	
1880	1887	1895	
1881	1888		
1882	1889		
	1890		

Victoria			1903	h	1911 q
1901 Ewd. VII	1896 a		1904 i	1912 r
1910 George V	1897 b		1905 k	1913 s
	1898 c		1906 l	1914 t
	1899 d		1907 m	1915 u
	1900 e		1908 n	
	1901 f		1909 o	
a	1902 g		1910 p	

George V			1923 h	1931 q
	1916 a		1924 i	1932 r
	1917 b		1925 k	1933 s
	1918 c		1926 l	
	1919 d		1927 m	1934 t
	1920 e		1928 n	1935 u
	1921 f		1929 o	The Britannia Standard Marks for 1927
a	1922 g		1930 p	

1936 Ewd. VIII			1943 H	1951 Q
1936 George VI	1936 A		1944 I	
1952 Eliz. II	1937 B		1945 K	1952 R
	1938 C		1946 L	1953 S
	1939 D		1947 M	
	1940 E		1948 N	1954 T
	1941 F		1949 O	1955 U
A	1942 G		1950 P	

24

		1963	h	1971	q	
1956	a	1964	i	1972	r	Eliz. II
1957	b	1965	k			
1958	c	1966	l	This sequence was discontinued after the 1973 Hall-Marking Act		
1959	d	1967	m			
1960	e	1968	n	1973	s	
1961	f	1969	o	1974	t	
1962	g	1970	p			a

		1982	H	1990	Q	
1975	A	1983	I	1991	R	Eliz. II
1976	B	1984	K	1992	S	
1977	C	1985	L	1993	T	
1978	D	1986	M	1994	U	
1979	E	1987	N	1995	V	
1980	F	1988	O			
1981	G	1989	P			A

			1781	I	1790	S
George III	1773	A	1782	K	1791	T
	1774	B	1783	L	1792	U
	1775	C	1784	M	1793	V
	1776	D	1785	N	1794	W
	1777	E	1786	O	1795	X
	1778	F	1787	P	1796	Y
	1779	G	1788	Q	1797	Z
A	1780	H	1789	R		

July '97 to March '80. The King's Head is duplicated.

			1806	i	1815	r
George III	1798	a	1807	j	1816	s
	1799	b	1808	k	1817	t
1820 George IV	1800	c	1809	l	1818	u
	1801	d	1810	m	1819	v
	1802	e	1811	n	1820	w
	1803	f	1812	o	1821	x
	1804	g	1813	p	1822	y
a	1805	h	1814	q	1823	z

			1832	J	1841	S
George IV	1824	A	1833	K	1842	T
1830 William IV	1825	B	1834	L	1843	U
	1826	C	1835	M	1844	V
1837 Victoria	1827	D	1836	N	1845	W
	1828	E	1837	O	1846	X
	1829	F	1838	P	1847	Y
	1830	G	1839	Q	1848	Z
A	1831	H	1840	R		

1849	Ⓐ	1858	Ⓙ	1867	Ⓢ	Victoria
1850	Ⓑ	1859	Ⓚ	1868	Ⓣ	
1851	Ⓒ	1860	Ⓛ	1869	Ⓤ	
1852	Ⓓ	1861	Ⓜ	1870	Ⓥ	
1853	Ⓔ	1862	Ⓝ	1871	Ⓦ	
1854	Ⓕ	1863	Ⓞ	1872	Ⓧ	
1855	Ⓖ	1864	Ⓟ	1873	Ⓨ	
1856	Ⓗ	1865	Ⓠ	1874	Ⓩ	
1857	Ⓘ	1866	Ⓡ			Ⓐ

1875	ⓐ	1883	ⓘ	1891	ⓡ	Victoria
1876	ⓑ	1884	ⓚ	1892	ⓢ	
1877	ⓒ	1885	ⓛ	1893	ⓣ	
1878	ⓓ	1886	ⓜ	1894	ⓤ	
1879	ⓔ	1887	ⓝ	1895	ⓥ	
1880	ⓕ	1888	ⓞ	1896	ⓦ	
1881	ⓖ	1889	ⓟ	1897	ⓧ	
1882	ⓗ	1890	ⓠ	1898	ⓨ	
				1899	ⓩ	ⓐ

Victoria	1900	a	1908	i	1917	S
1901 Ewd. VII	1901	b	1909	k		
1910 George V	1902	c	1910	l	1918	t
	1903	d	1911	m	1919	u
	1904	e	1912	n	1920	v
	1905	f	1913	o	1921	w
[a]	1906	g	1914	p	1922	x
	1907	h	1915	q	1923	y
			1916	r	1924	z

George V	1925	A	1933	J	1940	Q
1935 Ewd. VIII	1926	B	1934	K	1941	R
	1927	C	1935	L	1942	S
	1928	D			1943	T
	1929	E	1936	M	1944	U
	1930	F	1937	N	1945	V
	1931	G	1938	O	1946	W
	1932	H	1939	P	1947	X
[A]					1948	Y
					1949	Z

				1960	*L*		George VI
1950	*A*	1954	*E*	1961	*M*		1952 Eliz. II
1951	*B*	1955	*F*	1962	*N*		
		1956	*G*	1963	*O*		
1952	*C*	1957	*H*	1964	*P*		
1953	*D*	1958	*I*	1965	*Q*		
		1959	*K*				*A*

		1972	*X*				
1966	*R*						Eliz. II
1967	*S*	1973	*Y*				
1968	*T*						
1969	*U*	1974	*Z*				
1970	*V*						
1971	*W*						*R*

		1981	*g*	1988	*O*		
1975	*A*	1982	*H*	1989	*P*		Eliz. II
1976	*B*	1983	*J*	1990	*Q*		
1977	*C*	1984	*K*	1991	*R*		
1978	*D*	1985	*L*	1992	*S*		
1979	*E*	1986	*M*	1993	*T*		
1980	*F*	1987	*N*	1994	*U*		
				1995	*V*		*A*

	1680		1690		1690 to 1700

Charles II

1685
James II

1689
Wm. & My.

1694
William III

				1709	**I**	1718	**S**
		1701	**A**	1710	**K**		
	1702	**B**	1711	**L**	1719	**T**
	1703	**C**	1712	**M**	1720	**U**
	1704	**D**	1713	**N**	1721	**V**
William III 1702	1705	**E**	1714	**O**	1722	**W**
Anne 1714	1706	**F**	1715	**P**	1723	**X**
George I	1707	**G**	1716	**Q**	1724	**Y**
A	1708	**H**	1717	**R**	1725	**Z**

				1734	**J**	1743	**J**
		1726	**A**	1735	**K**	1744	**J**
	1727	**B**	1736	**L**	1745	**U**
George I	1728	**C**	1737	**M**	1746	**V**
1727 George II	1729	**D**	1738	**N**	1747	**W**
	1730	**E**	1739	**O**	1748	**X**
	1731	**F**	1740	**P**	1749	**Y**
	1732	**G**	1741	**Q**	1750	**Z**
A	1733	**K**	1742	**R**		

	1759	ⓘ	1768	Ⓢ	
1751 ⓐ	1760	ⓚ	1769	Ⓣ	
1752 ⓑ	1761	ⓛ	1770	Ⓤ	
1753 ⓒ	1762	ⓜ	1771	Ⓤ	
1754 ⓓ	1763	ⓝ	1772	Ⓥ	George II
1755 ⓔ	1764	ⓞ	1773	Ⓦ	1760
1756 ⓕ	1765	ⓟ	1774	Ⓧ	George III
1757 ⓖ	1766	ⓠ	1775	Ⓨ	
1758 ⓗ	1767	Ⓡ			ⓐ

	1782	⓰	1789	ⓞ	
1776 ⓐ	1783	⓱	1790	ⓟ	
1777 ⓑ			1791	ⓠ	
1778 ⓒ	1784	⓲	1792	ⓡ	George III
	1785	ⓚ	1793	ⓢ	
1779 ⓓ	1786	ⓛ	1794	ⓣ	
1780 ⓔ	1787	ⓜ	1795	ⓤ	
1781 ⓕ	1788	ⓝ	1796	ⓥ	ⓐ

	1803	Ⓖ	1811	Ⓟ	
1797 Ⓐ	1804	Ⓗ	1812	Ⓠ	
1798 Ⓑ	1805	Ⓘ	1813	Ⓡ	
1799 Ⓒ	1806	Ⓚ	1814	Ⓢ	
	1807	Ⓛ	1815	Ⓣ	George III
1800 Ⓓ	1808	Ⓜ	1816	Ⓤ	
1801 Ⓔ	1809	Ⓝ	1817	Ⓥ	
1802 Ⓕ	1810	Ⓞ			Ⓐ

			1824	F	1833	P
	1818	A	1825	G	1834	Q
	1819	B	1826	H	1835	R
George III	1820	C	1827	I	1836	S
1820 George IV	1821	D	1828	K	1837	T
1830 William IV	1822	D	1829	L	1838	U
1837 Victoria			1830	M		
			1831	N		
A	1823	E	1832	O		

			1847	J	1856	S
	1839	A	1848	K	1857	T
Victoria	1840	B	1849	L	1858	U
	1841	C	1850	M	1859	V
	1842	D	1851	N	1860	W
	1843	E	1852	O	1861	X
	1844	F	1853	P	1862	Y
	1845	G	1854	Q	1863	Z
A	1846	H	1855	R		

			1871	h	1879	q
	1864	a	1872	i	1880	r
Victoria	1865	b	1873	k	1881	s
	1866	c	1874	l	1882	t
	1867	d	1875	m	1883	u
	1868	e	1876	n		
	1869	f	1877	o		
a	1870	g	1878	p		

		1897	Ⓞ	
1884 Ⓐ	1890 Ⓖ	1898 Ⓟ		Victoria
1885 Ⓑ	1891 Ⓗ	1899 Ⓠ		
1886 Ⓒ	1892 Ⓘ	1900 Ⓡ		
1887 Ⓓ	1893 Ⓚ	An alternative sterling mark used since 1839.		
1888 Ⓔ	1894 Ⓛ			
1889 Ⓕ	1895 Ⓜ	An alternative date letter shield used since 1900.		
	1896 Ⓝ			Ⓐ

		1917	ℛ	
1901 Ⓐ	1908 ℋ	1918 ℐ		Ewd. VII
1902 Ⓑ	1909 ℐ	1919 ℐ		1910 George V
1903 Ⓒ	1910 ℐ	1920 ℐ		
1904 Ⓓ	1911 ℒ	1921 ℐ		
1905 Ⓔ	1912 ℳ	1922 ℐ		
1906 Ⓕ	1913 ℐ	1923 ℐ		
1907 Ⓖ	1914 Ⓞ	1924 ℐ		
	1915 ℐ	1925 ℐ		Ⓐ
	1916 ℐ			

		1940 Ⓟ		
1926 Ⓐ	1933 Ⓗ	1941 Ⓠ		George V
1927 Ⓑ	1934 Ⓘ	1942 Ⓡ		1936 Ewd. VIII
1928 Ⓒ	1935 Ⓚ	1943 Ⓢ		1936 George VI
1929 Ⓓ	1936 Ⓛ	1944 Ⓣ		
1930 Ⓔ	1937	1945 Ⓤ		
1931 ff	1938 Ⓝ	1946 Ⓥ		
1932 Ⓖ	1939 Ⓞ	1947 Ⓦ		Ⓐ

33

					1961	L
George VI	1948	N	1954	D	1962	M
1952 Eliz. II	1949	Y	1955	E		
	1950	Z	1956	F		
	1951	A	1957	G		
	1952	B	1958	H		
	1953	C	1959	J		
			1960	K		

In August of 1962 the Chester Assay Office closed.

		1645	H	1652	P		
				1653	Q		
1638	A	1646	I	1654	R	Charles I	
1639	B	1647	K			1649 Charles II	
1640	C	1648	L	1655	S		
1641	D	1649	M	1656	T		
1642	E	1650	N	1657	U		
1643	F	1651	O				A
1644	G						

		1665	h	1672	p		
		1666	i	1673	q		
1658	a	1667	k	1674	r	Charles II	
1659	b	1668	l	1675	s		
1660	c	1669	m	1676	t		
1661	d	1670	n	1677	u		
1662	e						
1663	f	1671	o				a
1664	g						

		1688–93	h	1704	R		
		1694–5	K	1706–7	S		
1678	A	1696–8	L	1708–9	T	Charles II	
1679	B	1699	M	1710–11	U	1685 James II	
1680	C	1700	N	1712–13	W	1689 Wm. & My.	
1681	D	1701	O	1714	X	1694 William III	
1682	E	1702	P	1715	Y	1702 Anne 1714 George I	
1683–4	F	1703	Q	1716	Z		A
1685–7	G						

George I	1717		1726		1736	
1727 George II	1718		1727		1737	
	1719		1728		1738	
			1729		1739	
	1720		1730		1740	
	1721		1731		1741-2	
	1722		1732		1743-4	
	1723		1733		1745	
	1724		1734		1746	
	1725		1735		An alternative Crowned Harp found between 1739 and 1748.	

George II	1747		1757		1766	
			1758			
			1759		1767	
1760 George III	1748				1768	
	1749		1760		1769	
	1750		1761		1770	
	1751		1762		1771	
	1752		1763		1772	
	1753		1764		An alternative Hibernia found between 1752 and 1754.	
	1754		1765			

		1781	🛡I	1790	🛡S		
1773	🛡A	1782	🛡K	1791	🛡T		
1774	🛡B	1783	🛡L	1792	🛡U		
1775	🛡C	1784	🛡M				George III
		1785	🛡N	1793	🛡W		
		1786	🛡O	1794	🛡X		
1776	🛡D			1795	🛡Y		
1777	🛡E			1796	🛡Z		
1778	🛡F	1787	🛡P				
1779	🛡G	1788	🛡Q				
1780	🛡H	1789	🛡R				🛡A

1797	🛡A	1806	🛡K	1815	🛡T		
1798	🛡B	1807	🛡L	1816	🛡U		
1799	🛡C	1808	🛡M	1817	🛡W		
1800	🛡D	1809	🛡N	1818	🛡X		George III
1801	🛡E			1819	🛡Y		1820 George IV
1802	🛡F	1810	🛡O	1820	🛡Z		
1803	🛡G	1811	🛡P				
1804	🛡H	1812	🛡Q				
1805	🛡I	1813	🛡R				
		1814	🛡S				🛡A

	1821	Ⓐ			
	1822	Ⓑ			
	1823	Ⓒ			
1820 George IV	1824	Ⓓ			
1830 William IV	1825	Ⓔ ⓔ			
1837 Victoria	1826	Ⓕ			
	1827	Ⓖ			
	1828	Ⓗ			
	1829	Ⓘ			
	1830	Ⓚ			
	1831	Ⓛ			
	1832	Ⓜ			
	1833	Ⓝ			
	1834	Ⓞ			
	1835	Ⓟ			
	1836	Ⓠ			
	1837	Ⓡ			
	1838	Ⓢ			
	1839	Ⓣ			
	1840	Ⓤ			
	1841	Ⓥ			
	1842	Ⓦ			
	1843	Ⓧ			
	1844	Ⓨ			
Ⓐ	1845	Ⓩ			

38

1846	â
1847	b
1848	c
1849	d
1850	e
1851	f f
1852	g g
1853	h h
1854	j

1855	k
1856	l
1857	m
1858	n
1859	o
1860	p
1861	q
1862	r
1863	s

1864	t
1865	u
1866	v
1867	w
1868	x
1869	y
1870	z

Victoria

â

1871	A
1872	B
1873	C
1874	D
1875	E
1876	F
1877	G
1878	H
1879	I

1880	K
1881	L
1882	M
1883	N
1884	O
1885	P
1886	Q
1887	R
1888	S
1889	T

1890	U
1891	V
1892	W
1893	X
1894	Y
1895	Z

Victoria

A

🛡	🦮	©	1902	Ⓖ	1909	Ⓞ
🧍	1896	Ⓐ	1903	Ⓗ	1910	Ⓟ
Victoria	1897	Ⓑ	1904	Ⓕ	1911	Ⓠ
1901 Ewd. VII	1898	Ⓒ	1905	Ⓚ	1912	Ⓡ
1910 George V	1899	Ⓓ	1906	Ⓛ	1913	Ⓢ
Ⓐ	1900	Ⓔ	1907	Ⓜ	1914	Ⓣ
	1901	Ⓕ	1908	Ⓝ	1915	Ⓤ

👑	🦮	🛡	1925	Ⓑ	1935	Ⓣ
	1916	Ⓐ	1926	Ⓛ	1936	Ⓤ
🧍	1917	ⓑ	1927	ⓜ	🧍	🛡
George V	1918	Ⓒ	1928	ⓝ	1937	Ⓥ
1936 Ewd. VIII	1919	Ⓓ	1929	Ⓞ	1938	Ⓦ
1936 George VI	1920	Ⓔ	1930	Ⓟ	1939	Ⓧ
	1921	Ⓕ	1931	Ⓟ	1940	Ⓨ
	1922	Ⓢ	1932	Ⓠ	1941	Ⓩ
	1923	ⓗ	1933	Ⓡ		
Ⓐ	1924	Ⓘ	1934	Ⓢ		

		1951	**J**	1960	**S**		
1942	**A**	1952	**K**	1961	**T**		
1943	**B**	1953	**L**	1962	**U**		
1944	**C**	1954	**M**	1963	**V**	George VI	
1945	**D**			1964	**W**	1952 Eliz. II	
1946	**E**	1955	**N**	1965	**X**		
1947	**F**	1956	**O**				
1948	**G**	1957	**P**	1966	**Y**		
1949	**H**	1958	**Q**				
1950	**I**	1959	**R**	1967	**Z**	**A**	

		1976	**l**	1987	*B*		
1968	**a**	1977	**l**	1988	*C*		
1969	**b**	1978	**m**	1989	*D*		
1970	**c**	1979	**n**	1990	*E*	Eliz. II	
1971	**d**	1980	**o**	1991	*F*		
1972	**e**	1981	**p**	1992	*G*		
1973	**F**	1982	**R**	1993	*H*		
		1983	**s**	1994	*I*		
1974	**S**	1984	**t**	1995	*J*		
1975	**h**	1985	**u**				
		1986	*A*			**a**	

	1552		1611		1643	
Edward VI	1563	IC	1617	IL	1644	A
1553 Mary	1570		1617	G	1649	GC
1603 James I	1576		1613–21		1651	IF
1625 Charles I	1585	M	1616–35	G	1660	VB
1649 Charles II	1589		1633	WA	1665	IS
	1591		1637	IS	1669	AR
	1591–4	VC	1640	T	1663–81	E
	1596	EH	1642	IF	1675	W
	1609	BR				

		B	1689	i		T
1685 James II	1681	a	1690	k	1698	S
1689 Wm. & My.		B	1691	l	1699	t
1694 William III	1682	b	1692	m	1700	U
1702 Anne	1683	c	1693	n	1701	W
	1684	d	1694	o		
	1685	e	1695	p	1702	x
	1686	f		P	1703	y
	1687	g	1696	q	1704	z
	1688	h	1697	r		

		Year		Year		Year		
🏰	🛡️	1713	**I**	1721	**R**	🏰	
1705	**A**	🏰	**EP**	1722	**S**	Anne	
1706	**B**	1714	**K**	1723	**T**	1714 George I	
🏰	**EP**	1715	**L**	1724	**U**	1727 George II	
1707	**C**	1716	**M**	1725	**V**		
1708	**D**	1717	**N**	1726	**W**		
1709	**E**	🏰	**EP**	1727	**X**		
1710	**F**	1718	**O**	1728	**Y**		
1711	**G**	1719	**P**	1729	**Z**		
🏰	**EP**	🏰	**EP**				
1712	**H**	1720	**q**				**A**

		Year		Year		Year		
🏰	**AU**	1739	**K**	1746	**R**	🏰	
1730	**A**	🏰	**CED**	🏰	**HG**	George II	
1731	**B**	1740	**L**	1747	**S**		
1732	**C**	1741	**M**	1748	**T**		
1733	**D**	🏰	**EL**	1749	**U**		
1734	**E**	1742	**N**	1750	**V**		
1735	**F**	1743	**O**	1751	**W**		
1736	**G**	🏰	**HG**	1752	**X**		
1737	**H**	1744	**P**	1753	**Y**		
1738	**I**	1745	**Q**	1754	**Z**	**A**	

43

George II	1755		1763		1771	
1760 George III	1756		1764		1772	
	1757		1765		1773	
	1758		1766		1774	
	1759		1767		1775	
	1760		1768		1776	
	1761		1769		1777	
	1762		1770		1778	
					1779	

HG

Alternative town marks sometimes found around 1771.

George III	1780	A	1789		1798	S
	1781	B	1790	K		
	1782	C	1791	L	1799	T
	1783	D	1792	M	1800	U
	1784	E	1793	N	1801	V
	1785	F	1794	O		
	1786	G	1795	P	1802	W
	1787	G	1796	Q	1803	X
	1788	H	1797	R	1804	Y
					1805	Z

A

🏛	🦁	1814	**i**	🏛	🦁	🏰
1806	**a** 👤	1815	**J**	1824	**s** 👤	George III
1807	**b**	1816	**k**	1825	**t**	1820 George IV
1808	**c**	1817	**l**	🏛	🦁	1830 William IV
🏛	🦁	1818	**m**	1826	**u** 👤	
1809	**d** 👤	1819	**n**	1827	**v**	
1810	**e**	🏛	🦁	1828	**w**	
1811	**f**	1820	**o** 👤	1829	**x**	
1812	**g**	1821	**p**	1830	**y**	
🏛	🦁	1822	**q**	1831	**z**	
1813	**h** 👤	1823	**r**			**a**

🏛	🦁	1841	**k** 👤	1851	**U**	🏰
1832	**A** 👤	1842	**L**	1852	**V**	William IV
1833	**B**	1843	**M**	1853	**W**	1837 Victoria
1834	**C**	1844	**N**	1854	**X**	
1835	**D**	1845	**O**	1855	**Y**	
1836	**E**	1846	**P**	1856	**Z**	
1837	**F**	1847	**Q**			
1838	**G**	1848	**R**			
1839	**H**	1849	**S**			
1840	**J**	1850	**T**			**A**

Victoria		1865 Ⓘ	1874 Ⓢ	
1857 Ⓐ		1866 Ⓚ		
1858 Ⓑ		1867 Ⓛ	1875 Ⓣ	
1859 Ⓒ		1868 Ⓜ	1876 Ⓤ	
1860 Ⓓ		1869 Ⓝ	1877 Ⓥ	
1861 Ⓔ		1870 Ⓞ	1878 Ⓦ	
1862 Ⓕ		1871 Ⓟ	1879 Ⓧ	
1863 Ⓖ		1872 Ⓠ	1880 Ⓨ	
1864 Ⓗ		1873 Ⓡ	1881 Ⓩ	

Ⓐ

Victoria 1901 Ewd. VII	1882 ⓐ	1890 ⓘ	1898 ⓣ
	1883 ⓑ	1891 ⓚ	1899 ⓢ
	1884 ⓒ	1892 ⓛ	1900 ⓣ
	1885 ⓓ	1893 ⓜ	1901 ⓥ
	1886 ⓔ	1894 ⓝ	1902 ⓜ
	1887 ⓕ	1895 ⓞ	1903 ⓡ
	1888 ⓖ	1896 ⓟ	1904 ⓤ
	1889 ⓗ	1897 ⓠ	1905 ③

ⓐ

		1914	Ⓘ			
1906	Ⓐ	1915	Ⓚ	1923	Ⓢ	Ewd. VII
1907	Ⓑ	1916	Ⓛ	1924	Ⓣ	1910 George V
1908	Ⓒ	1917	Ⓜ	1925	Ⓤ	
1909	Ⓓ	1918	Ⓝ	1926	Ⓥ	
1910	Ⓔ	1919	Ⓞ	1927	Ⓦ	
1911	Ⓕ	1920	Ⓟ	1928	Ⓧ	
1912	Ⓖ	1921	Ⓠ	1929	Ⓨ	
1913	Ⓗ	1922	Ⓡ	1930	Ⓩ	Ⓐ

				1948	𝒮	
1931	𝒜	1939	𝒥	1949	𝒯	Ewd. VIII
1932	ℬ	1940	𝒦	1950	𝒰	1936 George VI
		1941	ℒ	1951	𝒱	1952 Eliz. II
1933	𝒞	1942	ℳ			
1934	𝒟	1943	𝒩	1952	𝒲	
1935	ℰ	1944	𝒪	1953	𝒳	
1936	ℱ	1945	𝒫			
1937	𝒢	1946	𝒬	1954	𝒴	
1938	ℋ	1947	ℛ	1955	𝒵	𝒜

			Year	Letter
Eliz. II			1965	k
	1956	A	1966	L
	1957	B	1967	M
	1958	C	1968	N
	1959	D	1969	O
	1960	E	1970	P
	1961	F	1971	Q
	1962	G	1972	R
	1963	H	1973 / 1974 31st December	} S
A	1964	A		

			Year	Letter
			1986	M
			1987	N
	1975	A	1988	O
	1976	B	1989	P
	1977	C	1990	Q
	1978	D	1991	R
	1979	E	1992	S
	1980	F	1993	T
	1981	G	1994	U
	1982	H	1995	V
	1983	I		
	1984	K		
A	1985	L		

1570	1585		Eliz. I
			1603 James I
1571	1635 1675	1690	1625 Charles I
			1649 Charles II
			1685 James II
1575	1680	1698	1694 William III
1580			

1701	1709	1718	Anne
1702	1710	1719	1714 George I
1703	1711	1720	
1704	1712	1721	
1705	1713	1722	
1706	1714	1723	
1707	1715	1724	
1708	1716		
	1717		

49

		1733	i	1741	r	
	1725 a	1734	k	1742	s	
	1726 b	1735	l	1743	t	
George I	1727 c	1736	m	1744	u	
1727 George II	1728 d	1737	n	1745	w	
	1729 e	1738	o	1746	x	
	1730 f	1739	p	1747	y	
	1731 g	1740	q	1748	z	
a	1732 h					

		1757	I	1765	R	
	1749 A	1758	K	1766	S	
	1750 B	1759	L	1767	T	
George II	1751 C	1760	M	1768	U	
1760 George III	1752 D	1761	N	1769	W	
	1753 E	1762	O	1770	X	
	1754 F	1763	P	1771	Y	
	1755 G	1764	Q	1772	Z	
A	1756 H					

		1781	I	1789	q	
	1773 A	1782	I	1790	r	
	1774 B	1783	K	1791	f	
George III	1775 C	1784	L	1792	t	
	1776 D	1785	M	1793	u	
	1777 E	1786	N	1794	w	
	1778 F	1787	O	1795	x	
	1779 G	1788	P	1796	y	
A	1780 H					

1804	H

1811	P
1812	Q
1813	R
1814	S
1815	T
1816	U

George III

1797	A
1798	B
1799	C
1800	D
1801	E
1802	F
1803	G

1805	I
1806	K
1807	L
1808	M
1809	N
1810	O

A

1817	a
1818	b
1819	c
1820	d
1821	e
1822	f
1823	g

1824	h
1825	i
1826	k
1827	l
1828	m
1829	n
1830	o

1831	p
1832	q
1833	r
1834	s
1835	t
1836	u

George III

1820
George IV

1830
William IV

a

1837	A
1838	B
1839	C
1840	D
1841	E
1842	F

1843	G
1844	H
1845	I
1846	K
1847	L
1848	M
1849	N

1850	O
1851	P
1852	Q
1853	R
1854	S
1855	T
1856	U

Victoria

A

Victoria	1857	(A)	1864	(H)	1872	(Q)
	1858	(B)	1865	(I)	1873	(R)
	1859	(C)	1866	(K)	1874	(S)
	1860	(D)	1867	(L)	1875	(T)
	1861	(E)	1868	(M)	1876	(U)
	1862	(F)	1869	(N)		
(A)	1863	(G)	1870	(O)		
			1871	(P)		

Victoria	1877	(A)
	1878	(B)
	1879	(C)
	1880	(D)
	1881	(E)
(A)	1882	(F)

1681 a	1694 𝕆	1700 𝖚	Charles II
	1696 𝖖	1701 𝖛	1685 James II
		1704 𝖞	1689 Wm. & My.
1683 𝕮		1705 𝖟	1694 William III
1685 𝕰	1698 𝕾		1702 Anne
		1707 Ⓑ	
1689 𝖎	1699 𝖙		
1690 𝕂		1709 D	**a**

1717	1758 S	1785 S	George I
1728 S			1727 George II
1734 S	1763 E	1790 S	1760 George III
	1773 S S		
1743 S		1795 S	
1747 S	1776 O		
1756 S		1800 S	
	1783 S	1811 🏃	
1757	The makers' marks were stamped in duplicate on either side of the town mark up to 1800.		**S**

		1827	I			1837	S
George IV	1819 A	1828	J			1838	T
1830 William IV		1829	K			1839	U
1837 Victoria	1820 B	1830	L			1840	V
	1821 C	1831	M			1841	W
	1822 D	1832	N			1842	X
	1823 E	1833	O			1843	Y
	1824 F	1834	P			1844	Z
	1825 G	1835	Q				
A	1826 H	1836	R				

Victoria	1845 A	1853 I	1862 R
	1846 B	1854 J	1863 S
	1847 C	1855 K	1864 T
	1848 D	1856 L	1865 U
	1849 E	1857 M	1866 V
	1850 F	1858 N	1867 W
	1851 G	1859 O	1868 X
A	1852 H	1860 P	1869 Y
		1861 Q	1870 Z

			1879	**I**	1888	**R**	Victoria
1871	**A**		1880	**J**	1889	**S**	
1872	**B**		1881	**K**	1890	**T**	
1873	**C**		1882	**L**	1891	**U**	
1874	**D**		1883	**M**	1892	**V**	
1875	**E**		1884	**N**	1893	**W**	
1876	**F**		1885	**O**	1894	**X**	
1877	**G**		1886	**P**	1895	**Y**	
1878	**H**		1887	**Q**	1896	**Z**	**A**

			1906				Victoria
1897			1907		1914		1901 Ewd. VII
1898			1908		1915		1910 George V
1899					1916		
1900			1909		1917		
1901			1910		1918		
1902			1911		1919		
1903					1920		
1904			1912		1921		
1905			1913		1922		

George V	1923	**a**	
1936 Ewd. VIII	1924	**b**	
1936 George VI	1925	**c**	
	1926	**d**	
	1927	**e**	
	1928	**f**	
	1929	**g**	
		h	
	1930		
a	1931	**i**	

1932	**j**
1933	**k**
1934	**l**
1935	**m**
1936	**n**
1937	**o**
1938	**p**
1939	**q**
1940	**r**

1941	**s**
1942	**t**
1943	**u**
1944	**v**
1945	**w**
1946	**x**
1947	**y**
1948	**z**

George VI	1949	**A**
1952 Eliz. II	1950	**B**
	1951	**C**
	1952	**D**
	1953	**E**
	1954	**F**
A	1955	**G**

1956	**H**
1957	**I**
1958	**L**
1959	**M**
1960	**N**
1961	**O**
1962	**P**
1963	**R**

In March 1964 the Glasgow Assay Office closed.

c.1658 to c.1670	c.1685 to c.1694	c.1700	Charles II
c.1672 to c.1684	c.1696		1685 James II
			1689 Wm. & My.
			1694 William III

	1709	1716	1702 Anne
1702	1710	1717	
1703	1711	1718	1714 George I
1704	1712	1719	
1705	1713	1720	
1706			
1707	1714		
1708	1715		A

1721	1728	1735	
1722	1729	1736	
1723	1730	1737	George I
1724	1731	1738	
1725	1732	1739	1727 George II
1726	1733	Between 1721 and 1728, the shapes of date shields and lion passant marks often varied. The lion sometimes faced to the left.	
1727	1734		

		1747	H	1755	Q	
	1740 A	1748	I J	1756	R	
	1741 B	1749	I K	1757	S	
	1742 C	1750	L	1758		
George II	1743 D	1751	M			
	1744 E	1752	N			
	1745 F	1753	O			
A	1746 G	1754	P			

		1775	I J	1782	Q	
	1759 A	1776	K	1783	R	
	1760 68 B	1777	L	1784	S	
George II	1769 C	1778	M	1785	T	
1760 George III	1770 D			1786	U	
	1771 E	1779	N	1787	W	
	1772 F	1780	O	1788	X	
	1773 G	1781	P	1789	Y	
A	1774 H			1790	Z	

		1799	I J	1806	Q	
	1791 A			1807	R	
	1792 B	1800	K	1808	S	
George III	1793 C	1801	L	1809	T	
	1794 D	1802	M	1810	U	
	1795 E	1803	N	1811	W	
	1796 F	1804	O	1812	X	
	1797 G	1805	P	1813	Y	
A	1798 H			1814	Z	

1815 A	1823 I	1831 R	
1816 B	1824 K	1832 S	
1817 C	1825 L	1833 T	
1818 D	1826 M	1834 U	George III
1819 E	1827 N	1835 W	1820 George IV
1820 F	1828 O	1836 X	1830 William IV
1821 G	1829 P	1837 Y	1837 Victoria
1822 H	1830 Q	1838 Z	A

1839 A	1846 H	1855 Q	
1840 B	1847 / 1848 I/J	1856 R	
1841 C	1849 K	1857 S	
1842 D	1850 L	1858 T	Victoria
1843 E	1851 M	1859 U	
1844 F	1852 N	1860 W	
1845 G	1853 O	1861 X	
	1854 P	1862 Y	
		1863 Z	A

1864 a	1871 h	1879 q	
1865 b	1872 i	1880 r	
1866 c	1873 k	1881 s	
1867 d	1874 l	1882 t	Victoria
1868 e	1875 m	1883 u	
1869 f	1876 n		
1870 g	1877 o		
	1878 p		a

Eliz. I	1565	A	1569	E	1590	
1603 James I	1566	B			1595	
	1567	C	1570	F	1600	
			1571	G		
			1573	IJ	1610	
			1574	K		
A	1568	D	1579	P	1620	

James I	With variations		1630	G	1637	O
1625 Charles I	1624	A	1631	H	1638	P
	1625	B	1632	IJ	1639	Q
	1626	C	1633	K	1640	R
	1627	D	1634	L	1641	S
	1628	E	1635	M	1642	T
A	1629	F	1636	N	1643	V

c.1645

c.1660

c.1675

Charles I

1649
Charles II

1685
James II

c.1650

c.1665

c.1680

c.1655

c.1670

c.1685

1688

1689

1701

1691

1696

1697

George III			1782			1791		
1773			1783			1792		
1774			1784			1793		
1775			1785			1794		
1776						1795		
1777			1786			1796		
1778			1787			1797		
1779			1788			1798		
1780			1789					
1781			1790					

July '79 to March '80. The King's Head is duplicated.

George III 1820 George IV			1807			1816		
1799			1808			1817		
1800			1809			1818		
1801			1810			1819		
1802			1811			1820		
1803			1812			1821		
1804			1813					
1805			1814			1822		
1806			1815			1823		

🦁 👑	1830 [g]	1837 [r]	👑 George IV
1824 [a]	1831 [h]	1838 [S]	1830 William IV
1825 [b]	1832 [k]	1839 [t]	1837 Victoria
1826 [c]	1833 [l]	👑 🦁	
1827 [d]	👑 🦁	1840 [u]	🅐
👑 🦁	1834 [m]	1841 [v]	
1828 [e]	1835 [p]	1842 [x]	
1829 [f]	1836 [q]	1843 [z]	[a]
👑 🦁	1851 [H] "	1860 [S]	👑 Victoria
1844 [A]	1852 [I] "	1861 [T]	[A]
1845 [B]	1853 [K] "	👑 🦁	
1846 [C]	1854 [L]	1862 [U]	
1847 [D]	1855 [M]	1863 [V]	
1848 [E]	1856 [N]	1864 [W]	
1849 [F] "	1857 [O]	1865 [X]	
1850 [G] "	1858 [P]	1866 [Y]	
	1859 [R]	1867 [Z]	[A]

63

Victoria			1876	**J**	1885	**S**
	1868	**A**	1877	**K**	1886	**T**
	1869	**B**	1878	**L**	1887	**U**
	1870	**C**	1879	**M**	1888	**V**
	1871	**D**	1880	**N**	1889	**W**
	1872	**E**	1881	**O**		
	1873	**F**	1882	**P**	1890	**X**
	1874	**G**	1883	**Q**	1891	**Y**
A	1875	**H**	1884	**R**	1892	**Z**

Victoria			1901	**i**	1910	**s**
1901 Ewd. VII	1893	**a**	1902	**k**	1911	**t**
1910 George V	1894	**b**	1903	**l**	1912	**u**
	1895	**c**	1904	**m**	1913	**v**
	1896	**d**	1905	**n**		
	1897	**e**	1906	**o**	1914	**w**
	1898	**f**	1907	**p**	1915	**x**
	1899	**g**	1908	**q**	1916	**y**
a	1900	**h**	1909	**r**	1917	**z**

		1926	**j**	1934	**r**		
1918	**a**	1927	**k**	1935	**s**		George V
1919	**b**	1928	**l**			1936 Ewd. VIII	
1920	**c**	1929	**m**	1936	**t**	1936 George VI	
1921	**d**	1930	**n**	1937	**u**		
1922	**e**	1931	**o**	1938	**v**		
1923	**f**	1932	**p**	1939	**w**		**a**
1924	**g**	1933	**q**	1940	**x**		
1925	**h**			1941	**y**		
				1942	**z**		

				1964	**W**		
1943	**A**	1953	**L**	1965	**X**		
1944	**B**	1954	**M**	1966	**Y**	1936 George VI	
1945	**C**	1955	**N**	1967	**Z**	1952 Eliz. II	
1946	**D**	1956	**O**				
1947	**E**	1957	**P**				
1948	**F**	1958	**Q**				
1949	**G**	1959	**R**				
1950	**H**	1960	**S**				
1951	**I**	1961	**T**				
1952	**K**	1962	**U**				**A**
		1963	**V**				

65

			1974	G		
Eliz. II	1968	A				
	1969	B				
	1970	C				
	1971	D				
	1972	E				
	1973	F				

			1982	H	1990	Q
Eliz. II	1975	A	1983	I	1991	R
	1976	B	1984	K	1992	S
	1977	C	1985	L	1993	T
	1978	D	1986	M	1994	U
	1979	E	1987	N	1995	V
	1980	F	1988	O		
	1981	G	1989	P		

During this period several variations of this town mark may be found.

Eliz. I

			1568	**K**			
1562	**D**	1569	**L**	1575	**R**	
1564	**F**	1570	**M**	1576	**S**	
1565	**G**	1572	**O**	1577	**T**	
1566	**H**	1573	**P**			
		1574	**Q**	1582	**Z**	**D**

During this period several variations of this town mark may be found.

				1596	**o**	
1583	**a**	1592	**k**	1597	**p**	
1584	**b**	1593	**l**	1598	**q**	
1587	**e**	1594	**m**	1599	**r**	
1590	**h**	1595	**n**	1601	**t**	
				1604	**x**	**a**

		1615	**J**			
1607	**A**	1616	**K**	1624	**S**	
1608	**B**	1617	**L**	1625	**T**	
1609	**C**	1618	**M**	1626	**U**	
1610	**D**	1619	**N**	1627	**W**	
1611	**E**	1620	**O**	1628	**X**	
1612	**F**	1621	**P**	1629	**Y**	
1613	**G**	1622	**Q**	1630	**Z**	**a**
1614	**H**	1623	**R**			

67

Charles 1	1631	*a*	1638	*h*	1650	*t*
1649 Charles II	1632	*b*	1639	*i*	1651	*u*
	1633	*c*	1641	*k*	1652	*v*
	1634	*d*	1642	*l*	1653	*w*
	1635	*e*	1643	*m*	1654	*x*
	1636	*f*	1645	*o*	1655	*y*
a	1637	*g*	1649	*s*	1656	*z*

Charles II			1664	*K*	1673	*R*
			1665	*J*	1674	*S*
	1657	*A*	1666	*K*	1675	*T*
	1658	*B*	1667	*L*	1676	
	1659	*C*	1668	*M*	1677	*V*
	1660	*D*	1669	*N*	1678	*W*
	1661	*E*	1670	*O*	1679	*X*
	1662	*F*	1671	*P*	1680	*Y*
A	1663	*G*	1672	*Q*	1681	*Z*

			1689	*H*	1696	*P*
	1682	*A*	1690	*J*	1697	*Q*
	1683	*B*	1691	*k*	1698	*R*
	1684	*C*	1692	*L*	1699	*S*
	1685	*D*	1693	*M*		
	1686	*E*	1694	*N*		
	1687	*F*	1695	*O*		
A	1688	*G*				

(date letters, set 1)	1711 Ⓤ	1782 **G**
1700 Ⓐ	1713 Ⓥ	1783 **H**
1701 Ⓑ	*No records for the period 1714 to 1778.*	1784 **J**
1702 Ⓒ		1785 **K**
1703 Ⓓ	1778 Ⓒ	1786 **L**
1704 Ⓔ	1779 Ⓓ	
1705 Ⓕ	1780 Ⓔ	William III 1702
1706 Ⓖ	1781 Ⓕ	Anne 1714
1708 Ⓘ		George I 1727
		George II 1760
		George III
		Ⓐ

(date letters, set 2)	1795 ⓘ	1803 Ⓡ
1787 Ⓐ	1796 ⓚ	1804 Ⓢ
1788 Ⓑ	1797 Ⓛ	1805 Ⓣ
1789 Ⓒ	1798 Ⓜ	1806 Ⓤ
1790 ⓓ	1799 Ⓝ	1807 Ⓥ
1791 ⓔ	1800 Ⓞ	1808 Ⓦ
1792 ⓕ	1801 Ⓟ	1809 Ⓧ
1793 ⓖ	1802 Ⓠ	1810 Ⓨ
1794 ⓗ	1803 and 1806 sometimes faced right.	1811 Ⓩ
		George III
		Ⓐ

(date letters, set 3)	1820 ⓘ	1829 𝖘
1812 ⓐ	1821 ⓚ	1830 𝖙
1813 ⓑ	1822 ⓛ	1831 𝖚
1814 ⓒ	1823 ⓜ	1832 𝖛
1815 ⓓ	1824 ⓝ	1833 𝖜
1816 ⓔ	1825 ⓞ	1834 𝖝
1817 ⓕ	1826 ⓟ	1835 𝖞
1818 ⓖ	1827 ⓠ	1836 𝖟
1819 ⓗ	1828 ⓡ	George III
		1820 George IV
		1830 William IV
		ⓐ

Victoria	1837	**A**	1844	**H**
	1838	**B**	1845	**I**
	1839	**C**	1846	**K**
	1840	**D**	1847	**L**
	1841	**E**	1848	**M**
	1842	**F**	1849	**N**
A	1843	**G**	1850	**O**
			1851	**P**

1852	**Q**
1853	**R**
1854	**S**
1855	**T**
1856	**V**

William Abdy
London
1784

Robt Abercromby
London
1739

1740

Stephen Adams
London
1813

Charles Aldridge & Henry Green
London
1775

Colline Allen
Aberdeen
1748

1748

George Angel
London
1850

1861

1875

John Angel & George Angel
London
1840

Joseph Angel & John Angel
London
1831

Joseph Angel
London
1811

Joseph Angel
London
1849

Peter Archambo
London
1720

1722

1739

Peter Archambo & Peter Meure
London
1749

Thomas Bamford
London
1719

1720

1739

Joseph Barbitt
London
1703

1717

1739

Edward, John & William Barnard
London
1846

John Barnard *London* 1702	
1720	
1720	
James Le Bas *Dublin* 1810	
1819	
John Backe *London* 1700	
1720	
Harry Beathume *Edinburgh* 1704	
Hester Bateman *London* 1761	
1774	
1776	
1778	
1789	
Peter, Ann & William Bateman *London* 1800	
1800	

Peter & Jonathan Bateman *London* 1790	
1790	
Peter & William Bateman *London* 1805	
1805	
William Bateman *London* 1815	
Joseph Bird *London* 1697	
1697	
1724	
William Bond *Dublin* 1792	
George Boothby *London* 1720	
1720	
1739	

James Borthwick
Edinburgh
1681

Mathew Boulton
Birmingham
1790

Mathew Boulton & John Fothergill
Birmingham
1773

Thomas Bolton
Dublin
1701

1701

1706

Thos Bradbury and Sons
Sheffield
1832

1867

1878

1885

1889

1892

Jonathan Bradley
London
1697

Robert Breading
Dublin
1800

1800

John Bridge
London
1823

1823

1823

Walter Brind
London
1748

1751

1751

1781

Robert Brook
Glasgow
1673

Alexander Brown
Dublin
1735

George Brydon
London
1720

1720

William Burwash
London
1802

1803

1813

William Burwash & Richard Sibley
London
1805

C

John Cafe
London
1742

1742

William Cafe
London
1757

Robt Calderwood
Dublin
1727

1760

William Charnelhouse
London
1703

John Chartier
London
1698

1723

1723

Henry Chawner
London
1786

1787

William Chawner
London
1819

1820

1823

1833

Francis Clarke
Birmingham
1836

Nicholas Clausen
London
1709

1720

Jonah Clifton
London
1703

1720

John Clifton
London
1708

Cocks & Bettridge *Birmingham* 1806	C&B
Ebenezer Coker *London* 1739	EC
1745	EC
1751	EC
Lawrence Coles *London* 1697	Co
John Cooke *London* 1699	CO
Mathew Cooper *London* 1702	CO
1705	CO
1720	MC
Robert Cooper *London* 1697	CO
Thomas Corbet *London* 1699	CO
1699	CO
Edward Cornock *London* 1707	CO
1723	EC

Augustin Courtauld
London
1729

1739

Samuel Courtauld
London
1746

1751

Louisa & Samuel Courtauld
London
1777

Henry Cowper
London
1782

1787

Paul Crespin
London
1720

1720

1739

1740

1757

Joseph Creswick
Sheffield
1777

Thomas and James Creswick
Sheffield
1810

Thomas, James & Nathaniel Creswick
Sheffield
1862

1862

William Cripps
London
1743

1746

1751

John Crouch
London
1808

Francis Crump
London
1741

1745

1750

1756

W. & P. Cunningham
Edinburgh
c. 1780

1790

1790

Louis Cuny
London
1703

D

Thomas Daniel
London
1744

1775

1783

William Davie
Edinburgh
1740

1740

William Dempster
Edinburgh
1742

William Denny
London
c. 1697

William Denny & John Barro
London
1697

John Denziloe
London
1774

Isaac Dighton
London
1697

John Downes
London
1697

Nicholas Dumee
London
1776

John East
London
1697

John Eckford
London
1698

1720

1725

1725

1739

John Edwards
London
1697

John Edwards
London
1724

1724

John Edwards
London
1739

1753

Charles Eley
London
1825

William Eley & George Pierpont
London
1777

William Eley
London
1778

1785

1790

1795

1795

1795

1825

1826

1826

William, Charles & Henry Eley
London
1824

Elkington, Mason & Co.
Sheffield
1859

William Elliott
London
1813

John Emes
London
1798

1802

Thomas Evans
London
1774

1779

1782

F

John Farnell
London
1714

1720

Thomas Farren
London
1707

1739

John Fawdry
London
1697

1720

William Fawdery
London
c. 1697

1720

1720

Edward Feline
London
1720

1720

1739

Fenton Brothers
Sheffield
1860

1875

1883

1888

1891

1896

William Fleming
London
c.1697

Andrew Fogleburg & Stephen Gilbert
London
1780

1780

Thos Folkingham
London
1706

1720

William Fordham
London
1706

1720

Charles Fox
London
1822

1823

1823

1823

1823

1838

George Fox
London
1861

1869

George Fox
London
1891

Charles Thomas and George Fox
London
1841

James Fraillon
London
1710

1722

William Frisby and Paul Storre
London
1792

G

Daniel Garnier
London
1697

Robert Garrard
London
1802

1818

1822

1847

Francis Garthorne
London
1697

George Garthorne *London* 1697	
Dougal Ged *Edinburgh* 1734	
Pierre Gillois *London* 1754	
1782	
James Glen *Glasgow* 1743	
Elizabeth Godfrey *London* 1741	
John Goode *London* 1701	
Andrew Goodwin *Dublin* 1736	
1739	
Hugh Gordon *Edinburgh* 1744	
James Gould *London* 1722	
1722	

James Gould
London
1732

1739

1747

1748

William Gould
London
1732

1734

1739

1748

1753

Robert Gray & Son
Glasgow
1819

David Green
London
1701

1720

Henry Greenway
London
1775

William Gwillim
London
1740

William Gwillim & Peter Castle
London
1744

H

Hamilton & Inches
Edinburgh
c. 1880

John Hamilton
Dublin
1717

1720

Charles Hancock
London
1799

1814

Charles Frederick Hancock
London
1850

1850

1870

1870

John Hardman & Co
Birmingham
1876

Peter Harrache
London
1698

1698

Charles Hatfield
London
1727

1727

1739

Hawksworth Eyre & Co.
Sheffield
1833

1867

1869

1873

1892

1894

Robert Hennell
London
1773

1809

1820

1826

1834
(4th generation)

Robert & David Hennell
London
1795
(3rd generation)

Robert, David & Samuel Hennell
London
1802

Robert & Samuel Hennell
London
1802

Samuel Hennell
London
1811

Samuel Hennell & John Terry
London
1814

Henry Herbert
London
1734

1735

1739

Henry Herbert
London
1739

1747

1747

Samuel Herbert
London
1747

Samuel Herbert & Co.
London
1750

John Hodson
London
1697

William Holmes & Nicholas Dumee
London
1773

William Holmes
London
1776

Daniel Holy & Co.
Sheffield
1776

1778

Samuel Hood
London
1697

1720

Charles Hougham
London
1773

CH

1785

CH

1786

CH

Francis Howden
Edinburgh
1781

FH

I

Thomas Issod
London
1697

Joseph Jackson
Dublin
1799

I·I

John Jacob
London
1734

1739

1760

K

Charles Kandler
London
1727

Charles Kandler
London
1778

1778

Charles Kandler & James Murray
London
1727

1727

Charles Frederick Kandler
London
1735

1735

Frederick Kandler
London
1739

1758

Michael Keating
Dublin
1779

1792

1854

William Keats
London
c. 1697

William Keats
London
1697

1697

John Keith
Banff
1795

James Kerr
Edinburgh
1723

David King
Dublin
1706

1710

L

George Lambe
London
1713

Jonathan Lambe
London
c. 1697

Paul de Lamerie
London
1712

1732

1739

John Lampfert
London
1748

1749

Louis Laroche
London
1725

1739

Samuel Laundrey & Jeffery Griffith
London
1731

Thomas Law
Sheffield
1773

1773

John Lawrence & Co.
Birmingham
1826

Samuel Lea
London
1711

1721

Lea & Clarke
Birmingham
1821

Ledsam, Vale and Wheeler
Birmingham
1824

George Lewis
London
1699

Charles Lias
London
1837

John, Henry & Charles Lias
London
1830

John & Henry Lias
London
1837

1839

1843

1845

Henry John Lias & Henry John Lias
London
1850

1853

1856

Isaac Liger
London
1704

1720

Mathew Linwood *Birmingham* 1805	**ML**
John Lloyd *Dublin* 1771	**JL**
Nathaniel Lock *London* 1698	**LO**
1698	**LO**
1698	**LO**
Mathew Lofthouse *London* 1705	**QL**
1721	**ML**
Mary Lofthouse *London* 1731	**M·L**
Seth Lofthouse *London* 1697	**LO**
Edward Lothian *Edinburgh* 1731	**EL**
Lothian and Robertson *Edinburgh* 1746	**L&R** **HG**
James Luke *Glasgow* 1692	**IL IL**

William Lukin
London
1699

1699

1725

Ben. Lumsden
Montrose
1788

M

Mackay and Chisholm
Edinburgh
c. 1849

Mappin Brothers
Sheffield
1856

1859

1867

1867

1878

1883

1885

1889

1889

Mappin Brothers
Sheffield
1893

1894

John Newton Mappin
London
1882

1883

1884

1884

1885

1886

John Newton Mappin and George Webb
London
1866

1880

Jonathan Madden
London
1702

Mathew Madden
London
1697

Jacob Margas *London* 1706	
1720	
Samuel Margas *London* 1714	
1720	
Marshall & Son *Edinburgh* c. 1842	
Colin McKenzie *Edinburgh* 1695	
Lewis Mettayer *London* 1700	
1720	
Nathaniel Mills *Birmingham* 1826	
Richard Mills *London* 1755	
1758	

John Moore
Dublin
1729

1740

1745

Thomas Morse
London
1720

1720

Richard Morton
Sheffield
1773

1773

N

Robert Naughton
Inverness
1815

Anthony Nelme
London
1697

1722

Francis Nelme
London
1739

Samuel Neville *Dublin* 1808	SN
Newton & Son *Sheffield* 1881	NC
Henry Nutting & Robt. Hennel *London* 1808	HN RH

O

Charles Overing *London* 1697	DV

P

Padley Parkin & Co. *Sheffield* 1846	PP &CO
Padley Stanwell & Co. *Sheffield* 1857	PS &Cº
Mark Paillett *London* 1698	PA
Simon Pantin *London* 1701	PA
1717	PA
1720	PA

Thomas Parr *London* 1697	
Thomas Parr Jnr. *London* 1717	
1732	
1739	
1739	
John Parsons *Sheffield* 1783	
Humphrey Payne *London* 1701	
1701	
c. 1701	
1739	
Edmund Pearce *London* 1704	
1720	
William Peaston *London* 1745	

William and Robert Peaston
London
1796

Samuel Pemberton
Birmingham
1784

Edward Penman
Edinburgh
1706

James Penman
Edinburgh
1705

Phipps & Edward Robinson
London
1783

Mathew Pickering
London
1703

Peze Pilleau
London
1720

1720

1739

John Pittar
Dublin
1751

1778

1813

William Pitts *London* 1789	**WP**
Pierre Platel *London* 1699	**PL**
Philip Platel *London* 1737	**PP**
John Pollock *London* 1734	**I·P**
Thomas Powell *London* 1756	**TP**
1758	**TP**
Joseph Preedy *London* 1777	**I⋆P**
1800	**I·P**
John Pringle *Perth* 1827	**IP**
1827	**I·P** **I·P**
Benjamin Pyne *London* c. 1710	**PP**
c. 1720	**PY**

R

Phillip Rainaud
London
1707

1720

John Rand
London
1703

Samuel Roberts
Sheffield
1773

Samuel Roberts Jnr. & George Cadman
Sheffield
1786

1786

Roberts & Belk
Sheffield
1864

1864

1892

1869

1879

Patrick Robertson
Edinburgh
1751

John (later Lord) Rollo
Edinburgh
1731

Phillip Rollos
London
1697

1697

1705

1720

Philip Rundell
London
1819

1819

1822

Abraham Russell
London
1702

S

John le Sage
London
1722

1739

1739

A. B. Savory
London
1826

1826

1826

1826

1826

1826

1836

John Schuppe
London
1753

John Scofield
London
1778

1787

Digby Scott & Benjamin Smith
London
1802

1803

William Scott
Banff
1680

James Seabrook
London
1714

1720

Daniel Shaw
London
1748

William Shaw
London
1727

1728

1739

1745

1748

William Shaw & William Priest
London
1749

1750

W. & G. Sissons
Sheffield
1858

Gabriel Sleath
London
1706

1706

1720

1739

Gabriel Sleath & Francis Crump *London* 1753	
Benjamin Smith *London* 1807	
Daniel Smith & Robert Sharp *London* 1780	
1780	
1780	
Edward Smith *Birmingham* 1833	
James Smith *London* 1718	
1720	
1744	
Stephen Smith *London* 1865	
1878	
1880	

Paul Storr
London
1799

1807

1808

1817

1834

John Sutton
London
1697

Thomas Sutton
London
1711

John Swift
London
1739

1739

1757

James Sympsone
Edinburgh
1687

1687

Richard Syng
London
1697

1697

T

Benjamin Tait
Dublin
1791

James Tait
Edinburgh
1704

Ann Tanqueray
London
1713

David Tanqueray
London
1713

1720

Joseph Taylor
Birmingham
1812

Samuel Taylor
London
1744

Taylor & Perry
Birmingham
1834

Thomas Tearle
London
1739

Edward Thomason
Birmingham
1817

1817

William Townsend
Dublin
1734

1734

1753

John Tuite
London
1739

William Tuite
London
1756

Joseph Turner
Birmingham
1838

U

George Unite
Birmingham
c. 1838

Archibald Ure
Edinburgh
1717

V

Ayme Videau
London
1739

Edward Vincent
London
1739

W

Edward Wakelin
London
1747

John Wakelin & William Taylor
London
1776

1777

Joseph Walker
Dublin
1701

Samuel Walker
Dublin
1738

Thomas Walker
Dublin
1723

Walker Knowles & Co.
Sheffield
1836

Joseph Ward
London
1697

Samuel Wastell
London
1701

1701

Mathew West
Dublin
1776

Gervais Wheeler
Birmingham
1835

Thomas Whipham
London
1737

1739

Thomas Whipham & Charles Wright
London
1757

Thos. Whipham & Wilm. Williams
London
1740

Fuller White
London
1744

1750

1758

John White
London
1719

1724

1730

George Wicke
London
1721

1721

George Wicke
London
1735

Starling Wilford
London
1717

1720

1729

David Willaume
London
1718

1718

1728

1728

1734

Richard Williams
Dublin
1761

1775

Wilm. Williamson
Dublin
1773

1747

Joseph Willmore	
Birmingham	
1806	**J·W**
Thomas Willmore	
Birmingham	
1789	**T·W**
1796	**T·W**
John Winter & Co.	
Sheffield	
1836	I W
John Wirgman	
London	
1751	**J·W**
Edward Wood	
London	
1722	W·O
1722	E·W
1735	E·W
1740	EW
Samuel Wood	
London	
1733	S·W
1737	S·W
1739	S·W
1754	S·W

William Woodard
London
1741

John Wren
London
1777

Charles Wright
London
1775

1780

Y

James Young
London
1775

John Young & Co.
Sheffield
1779

1779

Pottery and Porcelain

The marks on pottery and porcelain are not regulated in the way that those on precious metals have been for so many years. Not every piece of pottery has a mark at all and the same mark may be found on pieces from different dates, factories and even countries. Imitations are common and genuine marks may be blurred and difficult to identify. Nevertheless, marks on pottery and porcelain can add useful information provided that they are approached with some caution and, most importantly, they are seen in conjunction with the knowledge that can be gained from the piece itself. If you want to be able to identify items of pottery or porcelain it is essential that you get to know something about the many styles and methods of manufacture that have appeared over the years. The Pictorial Glossary which follows (p.139–148) will provide valuable assistance in distinguishing one type of ware from another, especially if you spend time touching and handling individual pieces at every opportunity.

Porcelain

A translucent ware, usually white, which may be either of 'hard paste' or 'soft paste'. The original hard paste porcelain was first made in China and the earliest imports into Europe were as long ago as the 15th century. It is made from a mixture of China Clay (kaolin) and China Stone and fired at a very high temperature. Despite the popularity of porcelain, European manufacturers were not able to make it until the method was successfully reproduced at Meissen in the 18th century.

Soft paste porcelain contains an additional mixture of bone ash, steatite clay or some other substance, and is fired at a lower temperature. It is not easy to distinguish hard from soft paste porcelain without considerable experience in handling specimens of the two. On the whole hard paste porcelain has a more glittery glaze and the material itself is stronger.

Pottery

Essentially pottery is made of clay, but many substances have been added to give extra strength and many different types and styles of decoration and glazing have been used.

Earthenware is made of some kind of clay, is opaque and may be of any colour.

Creamware is an earthenware with a cream coloured glaze which might be mistaken for porcelain but that the texture and outline of the pieces is less sharp.

Stoneware is a type of earthenware that has been vitrified at a high temperature and is often semi-translucent in its thinner parts. It is strong, with sand or flint being added to the clay mixture.

Delft is an earthenware with a fine white tin glaze, made in the 17th and 18th centuries.

Majolica is a highly decorated tin glazed earthenware originally from Italy.

Faïence is another tin glazed earthenware.

Types of Mark

As the illustrations on pages 149–198 show, there are hundreds of different marks to be found on pottery and porcelain ware. However, there are only five main methods of applying the marks.

Impressed marks are stamped into the body of the soft, unfired clay, and are almost impossible to fake.

Raised marks, as the name implies, stand above the surface as in the case of the early Chelsea 'Raised Anchor' applied in the form of a tiny pad of clay.

Incised marks are similar to impressed marks in being applied to the soft clay before firing, but they are scratched into the surface rather than stamped in.

Underglaze marks were printed or painted onto the surface of the ware by hand before the glaze was applied. Until 1850 these marks were only applied in blue; later other colours were also used.

Overglaze marks were painted or printed onto the surface of a piece after the glaze had been fired. A relatively low temperature was required to fire them, and for this reason they are the easiest marks to fake.

Do Not Be Misled!

Manufacturers invented marks to enable their wares to be recognised, but they also copied marks from foreign originals, usually when the intention was to imitate or rival a particular style of Oriental or Continental decoration. Thus Worcester copies of Meissen carry the borrowed 'crossed swords' mark and pseudo Chinese numerals were applied to wares decorated in the 'Japan' style. At Coalport, pieces decorated in the French manner were occasionally marked with the 'hunting horn' of Chantilly. Moreover, when the little Lowestoft factory imitated Worcester porcelain decorated with underglaze blue, they often borrowed that factory's open crescent and, at second hand, its Meissen crossed swords.

Many early factories were haphazard in their use of marks and even at a later period, as in the case of Chamberlains at Worcester, it was common to mark only one piece of a service. Furthermore, a service was not made as a unit but in batches of cups, saucers, plates and so on, which were stored and taken from the shelves as needed. The result is that pieces from one service may have different marks.

Establishing Dates

Although, as we have seen, it is easy to be misled, there are some simple guidelines which will help to establish the date of a piece.

Printed marks only appeared at the beginning of the nineteenth century.

Pattern marks which include the name of the pattern were only used after 1810 and are often much later.

The diamond shaped registration mark was only used between 1842 and 1883 (see page 193).

'Rg No', meaning Registered Number, was used from

January 1884 onwards.

Marks incorporating the Royal Arms or the word 'Royal' are nineteenth century or later.

The words 'Limited', 'Ltd' and 'Trade-mark' date from the early 1860's onwards.

The word 'England' was only used from 1891.

The words 'Made in England' have only been used in the twentieth century.

Visual Index

On the following pages you will find a visual index to the marks you may come across on pottery and porcelain. The marks have been divided into groups in order to help you to find the one you want. The first group is of marks containing initials, illustrated in alphabetical order. The second group is of marks containing numbers, in numerical order. The third group is of marks containing words, in alphabetical order, and this is followed by pictorial marks, grouped according to basic shape. Beside each mark is the number of the page on which you will find a full description of the manufacturer.

Marks Containing Initials

196	195	152	153
163	163	152	153
163	170	152	153
163	163	197	153
197	164	197	197
	181	195	173
150	172	152	
150		197	163
164	150		163
164	182	151	195
197	165	151	162

Marks Containing Initials (cont'd)

162   169   154   156

197   154   156

177   165   180

175   177   197

163   177   197   153

153   197

169   157

196   173   196   195

165   197   196

166   163   154

197   154   156   154

129

Marks Containing Initials (cont'd)

163	195	149	162
163	150	158	162
163	153	188	154
158	150	183	194
171	150		163
170		196	163
	149	163	168
163	195	194	
197	163		150
197	163	162	197
	163	162	

130

Marks Containing Initials (cont'd)

163   Y   194   ⅄   -Z- 194   Z

Marks Containing Numerals

195   ①   163   2   195   ⑤   163   ⁊

195   ♈   195   ③   195   𝕃   195   ⑧

195   𝕃   195   ♈   163   🐜   163   ⌀

195   ②   195   𝕃   195   ⑥   181   🐟

195   ♈   195   ④   195   𝕃   159   ▦

195   𝕃   195   ♈   163   ✿

152   2   195   𝕃   162   W6

152   2   158   4   195   ⑦

131

Marks Containing Words

173

173

◄E►

◄B►

173

164
D. J. EVANS & CO.

184

152 COALBROOKDALE

◄F►

153

187

156

184 BRAMELD

160
COPELAND

180 FENTON STONE WORKS

155 BRISTOL

160

164 FLIGHT

◄C►

186

164 Flight

188 CAMBRIA

188 CAMBRIAN

164 Flight.

165 Chamberlains

◄D►

164 Flight & Barr

152
165 CHAMBERLAINS C Dale

◄G►

165

160 DILLWYN & CO.

156

Marks Containing Words (cont'd)

165 *George Granger Royal China Works Worcester*

154

159

165 *Granger Lee & Co. Worcester*

166 HARTLEY, GREENS & CO.

158 **POUNTNEY & CO.**

176

 — **N**

— **S**

— **H**

182 NEALE & WILSON

150 *Salopian*

166 *Hadley*

 — **O**

176

163 *R Hancock fecit*

156

— **W**

154

— **P**

182 **WILSON**

Pictorial Marks

163	162	162	152
155	162	150	155
158	162	150	188
162	175	168	195
162	175	169	195
162	172	171	196
149	151	170	196
195	151	160	196
153	172	182	196
149	151	176	196
151	189	162	196
151	168	194	196

134

Pictorial Marks (cont'd)

163   ⚓   195   ⚜   195   𝄐

151   ⚓   154   🏴   195   ♡

Hieroglyphics

Square devices

194   ☐   195   ⊞   195   ⊠   195   ✗

195   ⊡   195   ⊏   196   ◇   196   ⅊

Angular devices

194   △   195   ♟   194   ◈   163   ⚏

195   ⋈   163   ▷   194   ⚔   163   ⋈

195   △   163   ◁   196   ⋈   163   ⋈

195   △   195   ⋈   196   ⋈

195   △   194   ◇   196   ⋈

195   ✳   137   ◇   196   ⋈

135

Round devices

194		195		195		163	
163		195		163		149	
195		195		163		149	
195		195		163			
195		137		163			

Dotted devices

163		156		163		163	
163		156		163		163	
163		194		163		163	
163		163		163		163	
194		194		163			
163		194		163			

136

Miscellaneous devices

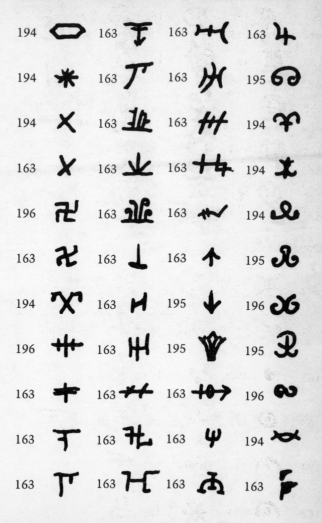

Miscellaneous devices (cont'd)

163	163	163	163
163	163	163	163
163	163	150	194
163	163	163	
163	163	163	

Pictorial Glossary

Agate Wares

Produced by a very specialised technique, the ware is usually associated with figures made by Astbury and table ware made by Whieldon between c. 1740 and 1750. At best, Whieldon's ware was made in solid agate, as the tankard here illustrated. Pieces were made by layering clays of different colour, doubling and slicing. Later wares were given a surface agate effect by painting, combing or mingling together several colours of slip (liquid clay) onto an ordinary clay body. This later process was used in the 1770's and 1780's by Wedgwood and Bentley in the making of a wide range of marbled effects.

Whieldon tankard 6" high, c. 1740–50

Belleek

The best known of the ware associated with the Irish pottery in County Fermanagh is that which was fashioned in traditional marine shapes. A speciality, however, was open-work baskets of the kind illustrated whose form was probably introduced by Staffordshire workmen familiar with creamware shapes. The mark upon this example is the standard printed mark of tower, dog and harp. It should be noted that this pottery is still in production and many of the patterns of the early period are still made.

Basket, 11" long, c. 1860–70

139

Biscuit

Derby group, c. 1795

Biscuit or bisque porcelain is a once-fired body without glaze. It is particularly suitable for figure making, since detail is not in any way obscured. Popular on the continent and in this country in the 18th century, it was used at Derby from about 1770 onwards. The best modeller was John James Spengler (or Spangler, son of the Director of the Zurich porcelain factory), who was at Derby c. 1790–1800. Biscuit figures were made during the early 19th century at several other factories, notably at Mintons. In c. 1846 a new body called 'Parian' was invented by Copelands while attempting to find the secret of Derby biscuit. Parian was used thereafter in preference to ordinary biscuit because of its creamier colour.

Black Basalt

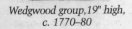

Wedgwood group, 19" high, c. 1770–80

Basalt or 'Egyptian Black' was used at many factories for the making of tea wares from about 1760, and in a much improved form by Josiah Wedgwood from c. 1773 to make classical figures, vases, plaques, etc. The improved stoneware body was smoother and a deeper black than that used, for example, by the Elers and Twyford. And it was ideally suited to fine modelling and engine turning. Wedgwood used it not only in its plain black form but also decorated it with unglazed enamels, relief ornamentation in red, and occasionally simulated the appearance of bronze by adding metallic powder to the mix.

Blue and White

Much of our earliest 18th century porcelain was decorated in underglaze cobalt blue, to imitate and rival the 'Blue Nankin' imported from China. At first the decoration, usually in pseudo-Chinese style, was painted, but by c. 1765 the process of overglaze printing, invented at the same time it would seem at Worcester and Liverpool, had been adapted to underglaze blue use. Much of this printed ware was made at Worcester, Caughley, Liverpool, Lowestoft and other factories. This plate, marked with the hatched crescent, is printed in the centre with the familiar 'pinecone' pattern, while the border is painted. The appearance of this early blue and white is entirely different from that of the abundant blue-printed domestic wares made at Spodes and elsewhere during the period c. 1780–1840.

Worcester plate, 7" diam., c. 1765–70

Creamware

Creamware was made as early as c. 1720, when Astbury added white clay and flint to his bodies. By about 1750 it was widely produced throughout the Potteries, as being a vast improvement on any other cheaply produced domestic ware and indeed a dangerous rival to porcelain. Though its ultimate development was due to Wedgwood, who by 1767 had surpassed all his rivals in this sphere, Leeds creamware, made under the proprietorship of Hartley, Greens & Co. was also very fine between c. 1780 and 1800. The piece illustrated is typical of the perforated ware which was made, each opening, like the Oriental 'rice-grain' porcelain, being made with a separate punch and not, as was later done at Wedgwoods, by a multiple tool.

Leeds cruet, c. 1780

141

Delft

Delft has a light, porous body covered with an opaque, white oxide-of-tin glaze upon which decoration may be painted in blue or polychrome. Its name is taken from the Dutch town of Delft, because its manufacture reached England from the Netherlands in the 16th century. In due course this settled into three main centres – London, Bristol and Liverpool. Most early Delft was decorated in Chinese styles, in a dashing, often crude manner which was enforced by the absorbent nature of the glaze. Because the ware had comparatively little strength and, as may be seen in this illustration, the glaze was apt to chip easily, it was dropped for the making of domestic wares in favour of the cleaner, lighter, durable creamware.

Lambeth posset-pot, c. 1700

Doulton Ware

The decorative stoneware made at Doulton's Art Pottery from 1871 onwards is notable for its fine design and the accomplished decoration for which students from the Lambeth School of Art were responsible. Each example bears the mark of the decorator as well as the factory mark and often the date of manufacture. Thus, from L to R, the illustration shows light blue slip decoration on a white body by Hannah B. Barlow, 1876, incised decoration filled in with cobalt blue on a white slip background by the same artist, 1875, and carved decoration with light blue and brown colouring by Arthur B. Barlow, 1873.

Various Doulton styles, 1873, 75 and 76

Exotic Birds

The so-called 'exotic birds' which are to be seen on many early English porcelains had their origin in the 'fantasie-vögell' invented in the 1770's at Meissen, and Worcester in particular. The painting of these incredible yet colourfully decorative creatures was developed to a remarkable extent. They were used in many different kinds of design, and are to be found in many distinctive styles, some being painted by London decorators and some by factory artists. The plate illustrated here, bearing the 'fretted square' mark, shows the characteristic Worcester combination of a scale-blue ground, upon which are gilt-scrolled reserves of birds and insects. It should be noted that this particular decorative style was often copied by Samson of Paris.

Worcester plate, 73/4"diam., c. 1768–76

Martin Ware

The Martin brothers were early representatives of what we now call 'Studio Potters' – others were Bernard Moore and William de Morgan – who produced salt-glazed stonewares of outstanding quality first at Fulham and then later at Southall. One of the brothers, Walter, was trained at Doultons' pottery at Lambeth, and indeed there is a strong similarity between the wares made at Lambeth and those made by the Martins. Their pottery is best known for the much prized jugs in the forms of grotesque, almost horrifying animals and birds. The vase illustrated, bearing an incised pattern of fish and sea plants on a fawn ground, is representative of the more restrained kind of Martin ware, and bears the full, incised, written mark together with the numerals 8–87.

Vase, 1887

143

Mason's Ironstone China

A very strong earthenware, patented by Charles James Mason in 1813, to meet the demand for showy, often gaudy ware by those who could not afford fine porcelain. Of this new body Mason made a wide range of dinner and dessert services, vases, jugs, and even fireplaces. The Chinese influence is usually present both in design and decoration. The Chinese landscapes of the pieces illustrated have transferred pink outline washed in with enamels, and while the vases are heavily gilded, the jug, instead has yellow enamel instead of the gold, a common Mason practice. It should be noted that a striking variety of the ware has fine gilding, or gilding and thick enamels applied upon a rich mazarine-blue ground, and that occasionally a piece may be found bearing panels of fine painting of landscape, flowers or fruit.

Vases and jug, c. 1813–25

Moulded Ware

Since so much pottery and porcelain was made in moulds, skilled modellers could not only fashion their own original designs, but were able at will to copy silver shapes and the designs used at other factories. While some early factories, such as Worcester, made great use of moulded forms from the beginning, others such as New Hall confine their attention to shape alone, with no attempt to decorative detail. Once thought to have been made at Longton Hall, the type of tea-pot illustrated here, with its crisp moulding of palm-trees and strawberry-leaves, has now been credited to Liverpool.

Liverpool tea-pot, 8" high,
c. 1750–70

Oriental Decoration

When European potters began to decorate on porcelain they were obliged to rely upon Oriental sources for their designs – they were venturing into unknown territory, with no past experience. Most styles were imitations of the Chinese, often but not always Anglicised. Use was also made of the often simpler designs, mainly in red, blue, green and gold, of the Japanese potter Kakiemon. Bow porcelain in particular was so decorated, but this fine Worcester vase, marked with an open crescent and made c. 1770, is painted with what Worcester called the 'old pheasant Japanese pattern' reserved on a scale-blue ground, with the usual scrolling in fine honey gold.

Worcester vase and cover,
c. 1770

Powdered Blue

Amongst all the types of painting in underglaze blue on 18th century English porcelain, powdered blue is particularly attractive. This ground colour, copied from the Chinese, was applied by blowing the dry pigment through a tube, closed at one end with gauze, over the moistened surface of the ware, thus giving the granulated appearance visible in the photograph. The reserves were of course masked during the process. The central reserve contains an exceedingly rare subject, in that the name of the factory responsible for its manufacture, Bow, is to be seen written on the base of the vase. It may be dated c. 1755–60. Powdered blue was also used at Worcester, Caughley and Lowestoft.

Bow plate, c. 1755–60

145

Pratt Ware

The name of F. & R. Pratt of Fenton is associated with a new way of printing in multicolours, each applied from a separate plate. This is seen not only on their well-known pot-lids, but also upon dessert services, tea-wares, mugs, jugs, etc. This kind of ware was shown at the 1851 Exhibition, for which event this bread plate was specially produced by Jesse Austin, the chief designer, after H. Warren's 'Christ in the Cornfield'.

Bread plate dated 1851

Pratt Ware

Another kind of popular Pratt Ware takes the form of moulded jugs, such as this 'Parson and Clerk', made between c. 1780 and 1800 by William Pratt of Lane Delph, father of Felix and Richard. The mark PRATT is sometimes found impressed, but similar jugs were made elsewhere. The high temperature fired coloured glazes Pratt used are quite distinctive.

Jug, 8" high, c. 1820

Salt-glazed Ware

By about 1720 Staffordshire potters had evolved a pottery which by reason of its lightness, thinness, durability and delicacy, was a fair substitute for imported Chinese porcelain. This was a white stoneware, high fired so as to become semi-vitreous, and glazed with salt thrown into the kiln at a temperature above 2,000 degrees F. to combine chemically with the silicate in the clays to form a durable sodium silicate glaze which has a characteristic, pitted appearance like orange-skin. At a later date, after about 1740, the ware was often gaily enamelled, but plain white moulded examples such as this are most attractive.

Staffordshire dish, c. 1750–60

Slipware

Slipware is the earliest kind of earthenware which can be considered to be characteristically English. It is so called because a creamy mixture of clay and water, called 'slip', was used for its decoration. Slip was either painted on in large areas, trailed in lines and dots from a quill-spouted pot, or 'combed' into the surface of the ware. Alternatively, as in this example, it was used sparingly and thinly to impart colour interest. The piece illustrated is a rare Pilgrim Bottle dating from about 1350, lead-glazed, with splashes of white slip and richly applied foliate ornamentation.

Pilgrim flask,
mid-14th century

147

Stone China

Stone china, as pioneered by Josiah Spode the Second, was the precursor of Mason's Ironstone China, being first produced in 1805 and quickly copied throughout the Potteries, under various names. Although of hard, clean appearance it is, of course, an earthenware whose smooth surface has been whitened by blueing. Spodes decorated with transferred patterns mostly in the Chinese style, though often translated into the English idiom. The outline was always printed in a colour suited to the washed-in enamels, in this case in sepia.

Spode plate, c. 1810–20

Stoneware

Compared with white salt-glazed stoneware, specimens of this kind, which was made at Fulham about 1760, may appear clumsy in the extreme. They comprise however an important class of English earthenware which was made in London, Nottingham and elsewhere from the 17th century onwards. The applied ornamentation suggests that the piece chosen for illustration was made for a bell-ringer whose initials B.H. it bears. As is usual with this kind of tankard the colour ranges from brown to buff, and the characteristic 'orange-skin' pitting of the salt glaze is clearly visible.

Fulham tankard, 8" high, c. 17650

Porcelain Marks

Belleek Pottery

Belleek, Co. Fermanagh, Ireland. Founded 1863.
1. Impressed or printed, 1863–80.
2. Impressed or printed, the standard mark 1863–91.
Continued in various forms. 'Co. Fermanagh' and 'Ireland'
added c. 1891.

1   2

Distinguished by a nacreous glaze often constrasted with the unglazed parts
of the Parian style body. Tea-wares (very thinly potted). Dessert and cabaret
sets, figures, and ornamental wares often modelled after marine motifs.
Great use of delicate shading in green or pink.

Bow China Works

Stratford, London. c. 1747–c. 1776.
1. & 2. Early incised marks.
3. Anchor and dagger mark, painted, c. 1760–76.
4. In underglaze blue, c. 1760–76.
5. & 6. Impressed marks of the 'repairer' Tebo, but also
found on other porcelain.

1   2   3   4   5   6

Usually sensible durable wares, in contrast with those made at Chelsea,
which catered for a more fashionable clientele. Much painted underglaze
blue decoration and use of Japanese Kakiemon designs and of the famille-
rose enamels of pink, pale green, pale opaque blue and aubergine (purplish
mauve). Good figures, at first crude and heavy, but neater after c. 1754,
when scrolled bases replaced plain ones.

Bristol ('hard paste' factory)

Founded by William Cookworthy c. 1770, later Cookworthy and Richard Champion, closed 1781.

These painted marks are found in many forms, with different painters' numbers.

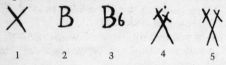

In common with Plymouth and New Hall they were makers of true porcelain, resembling white glass, with a thin, colourless glaze and a pale grey translucency. Often recognisable by 'wreathing' (the marks of the potter's fingers as he worked at his wheel) inside bowls, jugs, mugs, etc.

Caughley (or Salopian) Works

Nr. Broseley, Shropshire. Proprietor Thomas Turner, and later John Rose & Co. 1775–99.

1–3. Printed in underglaze blue on underglaze blue wares c. 1775–90.

4. Printed in underglaze blue on underglaze blue wares c. 1775–90, and not to be confused with the Worcester crescent.

5. Painted in underglaze blue on powder-blue wares c. 1775–90.

6. & 7. Impressed, usually in lower-case letters c. 1775–90, and sometimes accompanied by underglaze blue marks.

Pronounced CALFLEY, and until recently regarded as makers of rather inferior ware in the Worcester style. There has now been a wide reclassification of much of the porcelain made at the two factories, in the light of recent site excavations.

Chelsea Porcelain Works

Chelsea, London. c. 1745–69.
1. & 2. Incised c. 1745–50. Rarely with the year 1745.
3. The 'raised anchor' mark on a raised pad of clay
c. 1749–52. The anchor sometimes in red.
4. Small red anchor of the 'red anchor' period c. 1752–6.
5. Rare early mark in underglaze blue c. 1748–50.
6. & 7. Anchor in gold of the 'gold anchor' period
c. 1756–59, and sometimes found on Derby wares painted
at Chelsea c. 1769–75.
N.B. A large blue anchor is very occasionally found on
pieces painted in underglaze blue.

In its day, the English rival of Meissen and other Continental factories in
the production of elegant porcelain. Fine figures made from an early date,
often lovelier than the Continental originals from which they were copied,
but in turn much imitated by Samson of Paris, whose versions usually bear
gold anchor marks.

Chelsea-Derby

*William Duesbury of Derby purchased the Chelsea factory in
1769, and porcelains were decorated at Chelsea until c.
1784.*
1. In gold, and rarely in red.
2. & 3. In gold.

151

Coalport Porcelain Works

*Coalport, Shropshire, proprietors John Rose & Co., c. 1795,
and at Stoke-on-Trent c. 1926 onwards.*

1–4. Painted in underglaze blue on all kinds of ware,
c. 1810–25.

5. Impressed mark on flat wares c. 1815–25.

6. The Meissen 'crossed swords' in underglaze blue
c. 1810–25. Note that the same mark is found on
Worcester and Lowestoft porcelains.

7. In enamels or in gold c. 1851–61.

8. In enamels or in gold c. 1861–75, the letters denoting
Coalport, Swansea and Nantgarw. John Rose had
purchased the stock, moulds, etc. of the Welsh factories
c. 1820–22.

9. An early painted mark, also found in circular form,
c. 1805–15. Specimens may be seen in the Godden and
V. & A. Collections.

10. The crown mark c. 1881 onwards. 'England' was
added c. 1891, and 'Made in England' from c. 1920. The
date refers to the founding of the original earthenware
manufactory at Caughley.

N.B. The names 'Coalport' and 'Coalbrookdale' are
synonymous, and do not indicate that there were two
factories.

Always of excellent quality, particularly after the purchase of the moulds
and stock-in-trade of the Welsh factories, and the employment of
Billingsley. Most early wares were unmarked, but the names and work of
many of its Victorian artists, c. 1840–80, are known.

Derby Porcelain Works

The original works, founded c. 1750, closed in 1848, and a new one was started in King Street by former employees whose names appear in the marks used – Locker & Co., Courtney, and Stevenson Sharp, c. 1849–63. The factory was taken over by Stevenson & Hancock c. 1859. The marks of the modern Royal Crown Derby Porcelain Company Ltd., est. 1876 are self-explanatory.

1. Incised c. 1770–80, also occasionally in blue.
2. Painted c. 1770–82.
3. Standard painted mark, in puce, blue or black c. 1782–1800, and in red c. 1800–25.
4. Rare painted mark c. 1795.
5. Printed mark of the Bloor period c. 1825–40.
6. Printed mark of the Bloor period c. 1820–40.
7. Printed mark of the Bloor period c. 1830–48.
8. Painted mark of Stevenson & Hancock c. 1861–1935.
9. Printed mark of the modern company c. 1878–90.

N.B. The standard mark c. 1890 onwards is an elaboration of No. 9, with the words 'Royal Crown Derby' above the crown, 'England' or, after c. 1920, 'Made in England'.

The products of the Derby factories span the history of porcelain-making from c. 1750 to the present day, and in addition to the decorative styles peculiar to Derby, almost every type of decoration was attempted, especially under Duesbury, with an eye to commercial success. When the Chelsea, Bow and Longton Hall concerns were taken over, the manufacture of many of their characteristic styles was continued. No contemporary factory employed a larger or more expert staff of specialist painters, who decorated not only everyday wares, but the beautiful cabinet specimens for which Duesbury's factory is famous.

Liverpool

The wares of many 18th century potteries have not yet been fully classified, and are rarely marked, with the exception of porcelain made at the Herculaneum Pottery, c. 1793–1841.

1. & 2. Painted in enamels or in gold, probably by Seth or James Pennington c. 1760–80.

3. Painted, and probably a Pennington mark c. 1760–80.

4. & 5. Impressed or printed c. 1796–1833.

6. Impressed or printed c. 1833–6. The 'Liver Bird' mark is found in many forms.

7. Impressed or printed c. 1796–1833.

N.B. The full name of the factory – 'Herculaneum Pottery' – was probably used, impressed, from about 1822.

It should be remembered that because a Worcester potter named Podmore went to Liverpool to join Richard Chaffers in 1755, to introduce the kind of steatite porcelain made at Worcester, there is often a marked similarity between some Liverpool and Worcester of the 'blue and white' variety.

Longton Hall Works

Founded by William Littler at Longton Hall, Staffordshire; c. 1749–60.

Few pieces are marked, but the marks illustrated are occasionally found on early wares painted in underglaze blue.

It is interesting to reflect that as far as we know, this was the only porcelain making factory in the great potting centre of Staffordshire. Littler is best known as the inventor of the distinctive, vivid ground colour called 'Littler's Blue', which he first used upon earthenware before venturing into porcelain making.

Lowestoft Porcelain Works

Lowestoft, Suffolk, c. 1757–1802.

1. & 2. Copies of the Worcester crescent and Meissen crossed swords marks, in underglaze blue, on blue-and-white wares, c. 1775–90.

3. & 5. Examples of artists' marks, in underglaze blue, on blue-and-white wares c. 1760–75, usually painted near or inside the foot rim.

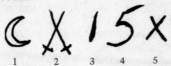

This small factory made mostly domestic wares, often of toy-like quality, simply decorated in underglaze blue painting or printing, or enamelled. At risk of repetition, it must be stressed that the factory was not responsible for the so-called 'Chinese Lowestoft' which was made in China for export to Europe. A great deal of ware has underglaze blue patterns similar to those used at Worcester and Caughley, and is often marked with the Worcester crescent or crossed swords.

Lund's Bristol

('soft paste' factory)

Redcliff Backs factory c. 1748–51, owned by Benjamin Lund, and taken over by the Worcester proprietors.

The mark illustrated, in relief, is very rarely found upon moulded wares, and may be coupled with the equally rare relief mark WIGORNIA on cream-jugs and sauce-boats made at the Worcester factory at the time of the take-over.

BRISTOL

Not to be confused with the 'hard paste' factory. It is most difficult to distinguish between Lund's Bristol (sometimes referred to as 'Redcliffe Backs') and very early Worcester, though the typical enamelled decoration found on some of it, of Oriental derivation, is recognisable by its jewel-like, dainty quality.

Minton

Stoke-on-Trent, Staffordshire, Est. 1793.

1. Painted mark on porcelains made c. 1800–30, with or without a pattern number below.

2. Incised or impressed on early Parian figures c. 1845–50, sometimes with the year cypher.

3. & 4. Examples of printed marks indicating the several partnerships, e.g. Minton c. 1822–36, Minton & Boyle 1836–41, Minton & Co. 1841–73, and Minton & Hollins c. 1845–78. C.f. Nos. 6–8.

5. The 'ermine' mark, painted, from c. 1850 onwards, with or without the letter M.

6–8. Examples of the numerous printed marks which incorporate an indication of the partnership (and period) and, somtimes, a pattern name.

9. & 10. Printed marks of the 1860's.

11. Standard printed 'globe' mark c. 1863–72. A crown was added c. 1873, and an S to the word MINTON. IN 1891 'England' was added below, and 'Made in England' c. 1902. See Year Cyphers, p. 194.

Naturally enough, early output consisted mostly of good quality transfer-printed earthenwares, and in the early 19th century the factory gained a high reputation largely due to the work of well-known painters, some of them from Derby. Among the wares for which the factory is renowned are white Parian figures, pâte-sur-pâte decoration on tinted grounds, fine almost eggshell porcelain, and 'Majolica' wares.

Nantgarw China Works

Nantgarw, Glamorgan, c. 1813–14 and 1817–22.

1. Impressed mark 1813–22. The C.W. (for 'china works')
is sometimes omitted, as is the space between the two
parts of the word.
2. Painted written mark c. 1813–22. The word may also
be stencilled, in upper-case letters, but cannot always be
relied upon as authentic.

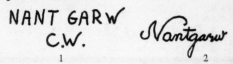

1   2

The factory, with Swansea, was at once the glory and the downfall of the
perfectionist William Billingsley. His soft-paste body was incomparably
lovely and wonderfully decorated, but ruinously expensive to produce.
Because he left Wales to go to Coalport, there is a real danger of mistaking a
superlative piece of Coalport porcelain for a piece of Swansea or Nantgarw,
and the collector has to learn the details of true Welsh shapes and artists'
characteristic styles, and to remember that the clinching Nantgarw mark,
impressed and impossible to forge, is often practically obscured by glaze.

New Hall Porcelain Works

Shelton, Hanley, Staffordshire, 1781–1835.

1. Painted pattern numbers usually in red or more rarely
in black, on 'hard paste' wares c. 1781–1812. Pattern
numbers appear commonly without the N.
2. Printed mark on bone china c. 1812–35.

1   2

Much New Hall porcelain was once called 'Cottage Bristol', and, in fact, the
Bristol hard-paste factory was taken over by a company of Staffordshire potters in 1781. From the outset, apparently, after production began in the
New Hall works, the decoration used was unlike anything done at Bristol
being slight and crude and applied to an inferior, greyer paste. The bone-ash
paste used later is much whiter and more whitely translucent. Although
most New Hall decoration is inferior, the factory was occasionally able to
produce a really elaborate, well-painted pattern, with gilding of high quality,
black-printing of the batt variety, and very occasionally printing in underglaze blue. The collector very quickly learns the distinctive moulded shapes
of tea-wares in particular.

Pinxton Works
Pinxton, Derbyshire, c. 1796–1813.
1–3. Though Pinxton porcelain is rarely marked, these painted marks are sometimes seen. The P is sometimes found without a pattern number. After William Billingsley left the concern c. 1799, his partner John Coke used the crescent and star mark, together with various arrow symbols, until c. 1806.

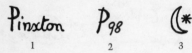

It may be supposed that here William Billingsley was first able to put his formulae to practical test, but in the more usual absence of marks the wares he made there are difficult to identify.

Plymouth Porcelain Works
Plymouth, Devon, under William Cookworthy, 1768–70.
1. & 2. Painted 'tin symbol' marks in underglaze blue or enamels c. 1768–70. Also to be found on Samson imitations.
3. Impressed mark of the 'repairer' Tebo, found also on Bristol, Bow and Worcester wares.

See the notes under Bristol, because William Cookworthy moved form Plymouth to Bristol in 1770, and in 1773 left the business to his partner Richard Champion.

Rockingham Works
Nr. Swinton, Yorkshire, c. 1745–1842.
Porcelain was not made here until c. 1826, and thereafter the standard 'griffin' mark was used, at first in red until 1830, and then in puce, with various alterations to the wording beneath. Thus: 'Royal Rockingham Works' instead of 'Rockingham Works' and/or 'China Manufacturers to the King' c. 1830–42, and 'Manufacturers to the Queen'

c. 1837 on. Very rarely an impressed ROCKINGHAM WORKS, BRAMELD or ROCKINGHAM BRAMELD is seen on porcelain c. 1826–30.

So much Rockingham porcelain is so lavishly and expensively decorated that the factory could not have survivied without the patronage of Earl Fitzwilliam. Unmarked Staffordshire porcelain is often called 'Rockingham', which is one reason why pieces bearing the 'Griffin' mark are held in high regard.

Spode

Stoke-on-Trent, Staffordshire. Josiah Spode c. 1784–1833, Copeland & Garrett 1833–47, W. T. Copeland & Sons Ltd. 1847 to the present day.

1. Early workman's mark, painted in gold c. 1790–1805.
2. A rare impressed mark on early wares c. 1784–1805, and in printed form c. 1805 onwards.
3. Written mark, usually in red, followed by a pattern number c. 1790–1820.
4. Printed in several styles, in puce or black on felspar porcelains c. 1815–27.
5. Impressed c. 1784–1805.
6. Printed c. 1847–51, and with the Cs elaborated 1851–1885.
7. Printed 1875–90.
8. One of the many self-explanatory printed marks of the period c. 1833–47.

(contd.)

5   6   7   8

Throughout its life the Spode factory, under any management, has never made anything of poor quality, and hardly any style of decoration has not been attempted. The collector is well-advised to visit the collections on view at the Stoke factory.

Swansea

Swansea, Wales, 1814–22.
1. Impressed, written or printed 1814–22. In the impressed form, may be accompanied by a trident or two crossed tridents to indicate use of the 'trident paste'.
2. Impressed, sometimes with the word SWANSEA, c. 1814–17.
3. Painted 1814–22.

N.B. No. 1 is suspect in printed form, because the copper plates used to produce it became the property of the Coalport concern in 1822, and it is possible that they may well have been used there to mark the particularly fine porcelain made to Billingsley's recipes.

SWANSEA   DILLWYN & CO.
1   2

Swansea
3

Much Swansea may be approximately dated by the kind of paste used, since Billingsley was obliged to make repeated efforts to save expense owing to kiln losses. Thus, in about 1816 the 'duck-egg' paste, greenly translucent, was introduced, to be followed shortly afterwards by the still cheaper 'trident body', which did not please the London china dealers.

Josiah Wedgwood & Sons Ltd.

Burslem c. 1759, Etruria c. 1769, Barlaston 1940.

1. Printed, very small, in red, blue or gold on bone china c. 1812–22.

2. Printed mark of the 'Portland Vase' from c. 1878. 'ENGLAND' added below from 1891. A similar mark, but with the body of the vase left white, and with three stars beneath it, was used from c. 1900. The words BONE CHINA were added c. 1920 and in 1962 the body of the vase was again filled in.

WEDGWOOD

1   2

Josiah Wedgwood was a perfectionist, and from the beginning the name of Wedgwood has always been synonymous with quality, so that while many Staffordshire potters imitated, for example, his jasper and cream ware, their products were for the most part of poorer quality.

Worcester

For convenience sake the marks of all the various factories and companies in Worcester are placed together. Their dates are as follows:

THE MAIN FACTORY, *c. 1751.*
First (or Dr. Wall) Period, *1751–1783.*
Davis/Flight or Middle Period, *1776–1793.*
Barr and Flight & Barr Period, *1792–1807.*
Barr Flight & Barr Period, *1807–13.*
Flight Barr & Barr Period, *1813–40.*
CHAMBERLAINS & CO., *c. 1786–1852.*
KERR & BINNS, *1852–62.*
GRAINGERS, *c. 1812–1902.*
HADLEYS, *1896–1905.*
LOCKES, *1895–1904.*
WORCESTER ROYAL PORCELAIN CO., *1862 to present day.*

Worcester
FIRST PERIOD
1–4. Crescent marks c. 1755–90, in underglaze blue.
1. Open painted crescent found on wares painted in
underglaze blue, or may rarely be found on enamelled
wares, in gold or enamel.
2–4. Printed, on wares in underglaze blue. Several other
capital letters are found inside the crescent, which may
also be found, rarely, in the shape of a face. Continued
into the Davis/Flight period.

5. The fretted square, painted in underglaze blue
c. 1755–1770 on wares painted in underglaze blue, in
several similar forms. Rarely accompanied by the crescent.
6–9. Painted or printed, according to whether the piece is
painted or printed in underglaze blue, c. 1755–70.

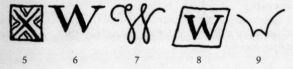

10 & 11. Pseudo-Chinese marks painted in underglaze
blue, many variations, c. 1753–70.
12–14. The Meissen 'crossed swords', painted in underglaze blue, usually found on wares painted in the Meissen
style, c. 1760–70, but also found on pieces printed overglaze in puce enamel.

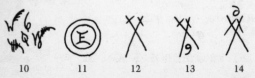

Worcester

First period (contd.).

15–17. On pieces printed in overglaze enamel. The RH refers to the engraver and printer Robert Hancock, and the anchor is the rebus of Richard Holdship, a former proprietor of the factory.

RH ⚓ *Worcester*	**RH** *Worcester* ⚓	*R Hancock fecit*
15	16	17

18. Examples of numbers disguised as Chinese characters, and so known as 'disguised numerals', found on wares made c. 1775–90, printed in underglaze blue on certain types of blue-printed wares formerly attributed to the Caughley factory.

18

18. Examples of workmen's or painters' marks painted on early underglaze blue-painted wares c. 1751–65.

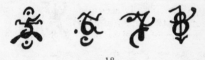

19

Worcester

DAVIS/FLIGHT PERIOD, 1783–93.
20. Painted in blue, 1783–8. A crescent alone, smaller than that used during the First Period, is also found.
21. A crown was added after the King's visit in 1788.
22. Found in various forms, painted in blue.

20   21   22

BARR AND FLIGHT & BARR PERIOD, c. 1793–1807.
23. Incised, usually on tea-wares.
24. Written mark found in various forms. Also, several self-explanatory painted or printed marks.

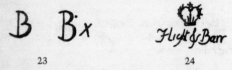

23   24

BARR FLIGHT & BARR PERIOD, c. 1807–13.
25. Impressed, often accompanied by self-explanatory written or printed marks, sometimes with London addresses and Royal warrant.

25

FLIGHT BARR & BARR PERIOD, c. 1813–40.
26. Impressed, and also as above.

26

Worcester
CHAMBERLAINS

27. Early mark, c. 1786–1810, found in many forms.

Between c. 1811 and 1840 many self-explanatory printed and written marks were used, some with London addresses, Royal warrants and crowns. Note that the words 'Regent China' denote a special body or paste used for expensive wares, c. 1811–20.

28. Impressed or printed, with or without 'Worcester', c. 1847–50.

29. Printed, c. 1850–2.

28

29

KERR & BINNS PERIOD, 1852–62.

30. Printed or impressed. The crown added in 1862.

31. Shield mark c. 1854–62. The last two numerals of the year in the central bar, the artist's initials or signature in the bottom L.H. corner.

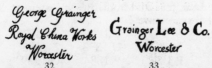
30

31

GRAINGERS, c. 1812–1902.

Grainger, Lee & Co. c. 1812–c. 1839, then George Grainger & Co. c. 1839–1902.

32. In several painted or printed forms.

33. Painted or printed in several forms, c. 1812–39.

34. Printed or impressed, c. 1870–89.

32

33

34

The same form of mark with 'Royal China Works' above and 'Worcester' below, was used c. 1889–1902, and the word 'England' was added from 1891, when date letters were also added below, commencing with A.

Worcester

HADLEYS, 1896–1905.

35. Incised or impressed on pieces modelled by James Hadley for the Worcester Royal Porcelain Company, c. 1875–94.

36. Printed or impressed, 1896–97.

37. Printed, Aug. 1902–June 30th, 1905.

Various other self-explanatory marks also used.

LOCKES, 1895–1904.

Founded by Edward Locke in the Shrub Hill Works, to make porcelain in the Royal Worcester style, and closed after a law action with the Royal Worcester company.

38. Printed mark, c. 1895–1900.

38

WORCESTER ROYAL PORCELAIN COMPANY,
1862–present day

The Flight Barr and Barr concern amalgamated with Chamberlains in 1840, and in 1852 reorganisation resulted in the foundation of a new company known as Kerr and Binns. When Kerr retired in 1862 the modern W.R.P.C. was formed. Note that Graingers were takn over in 1889 and Hadleys in 1905.

THE STANDARD MARK

1862–75. The standard Kerr and Binns mark (30) was taken over, with an open crown above and a C in the centre instead of a crescent. Two numerals below denote the last two numerals of the year, and from 1867 a system of date letters was used, as follows:

A 1867	G 1872	M 1877	T 1882	Y 1887
B 1868	H 1873	N 1878	U 1883	Z 1888
C 1869	I 1874	P 1879	V 1884	O 1889
D 1870	K 1875	R 1880	W 1885	a 1890
E 1871	L 1876	S 1881	X 1886	

Worcester

Worcester Royal Porcelain Company (contd.).

1876–91. The same mark, but with a crescent replacing the C in the centre, and the crown filled in. Year letters commencing with 'a' for 1890, as above.

This mark is also found in impressed form, without year letters.

1891 onwards. The same mark, with 'Royal Worcester, England' added. 'Made in England' denotes a 20th century origin.

A complicated system of arrangements of dots to denote year of manufacture was adopted from 1892, which may be referred to in G. A. Godden's 'Encyclopaedia' of marks. The standard mark has been revised from time to time, but is always self-explanatory.

Much of the early ware is unmarked, and even later, at Chamberlains and at Flights, the only mark on a service may be inside a tea-pot lid, sucrier cover, or beneath a single dish of a dinner or dessert service. The earliest 'blue and white' may bear either a workman's mark or a crescent, W or fretted square. With few exceptions it is unusual to find a mark on First Period enamelled pieces which have no underglaze blue in their decoration, probably because the painter who applied the underglaze blue could conveniently also apply the mark in the same colour.

Earthenware

William Adams & Sons (Potters) Ltd.

This concern, also known under several earlier titles, is perhaps the best known of the many Adams firms working in the Potteries during the 18th and 19th centuries. Founded c. 1769.

1. Impressed, 1787–1805 on Jasper wares, 1800–64 on earthenwares, with '& Co.' 1769–1800. Also on Parian figures 1845–64.
2. Printed, from 1896 onwards.
3. Printed, with pattern name, 1819–64. The initials below are found as a part of many other printed marks.
4. Printed mark on wares made for the American market c. 1830–50.

The finest Adams product is perhaps the blue jasper ware, violet toned, and often less frigidly modelled than the Wedgwood variety which it imitated. It should be remembered that William Adams was a friend and favourite pupil of Wedgwood and a modeller of exceptional merit.

Edward Asbury & Co.

Longton, 1875–1925.
Printed mark 1875–1925.
Also found with the names ASBURY and LONGTON.

H. Aynsley & Co. Ltd.
Longton. 1873 onwards.
An example of the Staffordshire Knot mark used by many
potters, usually with distinguishing initials similarly
arranged, and with ENGLAND added from 1891 onwards.

Another Aynsley, named John, had a pottery in Longton from about 1864,
making mostly porcelain but also lustre wares, bearing self-explanatory
marks incorporating only the surname.

J. & M. P. Bell & Co. Ltd.
Glasgow Pottery. 1842–1928.
1. & 2. Impressed or printed, with the addition of LTD or
LD from 1881.

1

2

Belle Vue Pottery
Hull. Various proprietors from c. 1802.
The 'Two Bells' mark, printed or impressed c. 1826–41.
The original partnership was between Jeremiah and James Smith and Job
Ridgway, until 1804 when Ridgway retired. The chief productions were
domestic earthenware, green-glazed and blue-printed ware.

Bishop & Stonier Ltd.
Hanley. 1891–1939. Formerly Powell, Bishop & Stonier.
Printed mark 1880–1936, after which date it was
impressed. The initials B & S were also used in printed or
impressed form, and there are several later (after c. 1899)
self-explanatory printed marks.

Booths Limited
Tunstall. 1891–1948.
Printed mark found on earthenware reproductions of First
Period Worcester 'blue and white' porcelains. The fretted
square of the same factory is also sometimes found.
Enamelled reproductions are not commonly marked.

Booth reproductions are remarkably accurate as regards decoration, but are
betrayed by their natural opacity, and, in the case of larger pieces such as
openwork baskets in the enamelled Worcester style, by creaminess of paste
and lightness of weight.

Bristol. Pountney & Co. Ltd.
c. 1849 onwards.
1. & 2. 1849–1889, and ohter marks incorporating initials
or names.
3. 1884 on pieces specially glazed. The numerals below
indicate month and year of manufacture. Ltd. added after
1889.

P. & CO.   POUNTNEY & CO.   BRISTOL
                                          +
                                          2/84
1   2   3

(contd.)

170

Cream-ware was first made in Bristol in about 1786, by Joseph Ring, who engaged potters from Shelton in the Potteries. Notable flower-painters were William Fifield (1777–1857) and his son John, who continued to work with the Pountneys. Many pieces, brightly painted by them for Pountney and Allies, including distinctive small barrels, bear the name and date of the person for whom they were made.

Bristol. Pountney & Allies

c. 1816–35.
1. & 2. Printed, impressed or painted, c. 1816–35.
3. Impressed, c. 1816–35.
4. Printed in blue, c. 1825.
5. Impressed 1816–35.
6. Printed in blue. 1830.

1

BRISTOL POTTERY

2

3

4   5   6

Britannia Pottery Co. Ltd.

Glasgow, formerly Cochran & Fleming. 1896–1935.
Several forms of the printed seated Britannia mark, side-face or full-face, 1896–1920. Later forms have self-explanatory lettering.

There were in fact many late 19th century potteries in Glasgow, all making the usual ironstones, cream-ware, stoneware and general domestic ware of the period.

Brown Westhead, Moore & Co.

Hanley. 1862–1904.

Printed mark 1862 onwards. The initials, or the name in full, are found in various printed or impressed marks, sometimes with a pattern name. The word CAULDRON appears in marks used c. 1890.

They were the successors, after many partnerships, to the Ridgways – Job, John and William – who began business in 1802. W. Moore had been assistant to John Ridgway. The earthenwares, Majolica, and Parian wares won the highest awards at many Exhibitions throughout the world, being, in the words of J. F. Blacker, 'peculiarly good, hard, compact and durable, and the patterns chaste and effective'. Note that old Cauldron ware was marked iwth such marks as I. RIDGWAY, RIDGWAY & SONS and JOHN RIDGWAY & CO.

Davenport

Longport. c. 1793–1887.

1. & 2. Impressed, the name sometimes accompanied by an anchor. Lower case letters 1793–1810, upper case letters after 1805.

3. Printed on stone china, c. 1805–20.

4. Printed c. 1795, sometimes with LONGPORT instead of DAVENPORT. A later version was used up to about 1860, sometimes with the last two numerals of the year on either side of the anchor.

5. Impressed, on wares of all periods. Many other Davenport marks are self-explanatory.

John Davenport was an artistic potter, and is better known for his porcelain, which bears similar marks to those reproduced here. His blue-printed earthenwares are particularly fine, with perforated rims to plates and dishes, and he made stone china in the Mason style, as, for example, his octagonal jugs. Decoration is usually strong in colour, with occasional fine gilding, and some excellent painting of fruit was done, probably by Steele of Derby.

William de Morgan
Chelsea, Fulham, etc. London. c. 1872–1907.
1. An example of the several name marks used c. 1882
onwards. '& Co.' added after 1888.
2. Impressed or painted, 1882 onwards.

1   2

William de Morgan may be classed with Bernard Moore and W. Howson
Taylor of 'Ruskin' fame as a studio potter who was inspired by the brilliant
strength of colour of ancient Continental or Oriental wares, in de Morgan's
case by the fine lustre effects on old Majolica and the intense blues of old
Persian wares.

J. Dimmock & Co.
Hanley. 1862–1904.
1. Printed monogram mark, 1862–78; sometimes the
same initials are found with pattern names.
2–4. Printed, c. 1878–1904. From c. 1878 the name of the
new proprietor D. D. Cliff was used in many printed
marks.

This firm originated in about 1816, when the son of Wedgwood's modeller,
Hackwood, entered into partnership with John Dimmock to make earthenware.

173

Don Pottery
Swinton, Yorkshire. 1790–1893.
1. Impressed or painted c. 1790–1830.
2. Impressed or painted, 1820–34. Another version bears the words GREEN DON POTTERY.

DON POTTERY

1

2

An almost unknown pottery until about 1800, when one of the brothers Green, of Leeds, became owner, so that many of the finest pieces made at Swinton were in fact of Leeds design.

Doulton & Co. Ltd.
Lambeth and Burslem. c. 1858–1956. The Lambeth works closed in 1956, while the Burslem works continued.
1. Impressed, c. 1858 onwards. The same words are sometimes found impressed in an oval or, rarely, in a circle, with the year of manufacture between them.
2. & 7. Painted or impressed c. 1882–1902, with ENGLAND after 1891.
3. Impressed or printed, c. 1887–1900.
4. Impressed c. 1881–1912, with ENGLAND after 1891.
5. Impressed or printed c. 1872 onwards.
6. Impressed, c. 1888–98.
8. The standard impressed Doulton mark, found in several forms from c. 1902 onwards. MADE IN ENGLAND added in 1891.

1   2   3   4

DOULTON LAMBETH

(contd.)

5   6   7   8

The revival of artistic stoneware was begun by Henry Doulton, the intention being to make domestic vessels as ornamental as the old Flemish ware. Actually a stoneware works was founded by John Doulton at Vauxhall in 1815, afterwards being carried on by Doulton and Watts before being transferred to High Street, Lambeth, some years later. At the 1851 Exhibition the Lambeth terra-cotta wares were highly commended, but it was some 20 years later that the use of sgraffito (scratched) designs typical of Doulton ware were developed, while different coloured bodies were gradually introduced. Nineteenth century Doulton ware may be divided roughly into the following classes: salt-glazed stoneware, usually simply called 'Doulton Ware'; chiné ware (faience either salt or lead-glazed), silicon ware, which is vitrified stoneware without a salt glaze, but making use of coloured clays; Carrara Ware which is covered with a transparent crystalline enamel; marqueterie ware made of marbled clays in chequered designs; Lambeth faience which is a terra-cotta or biscuit body bearing underglaze painting, and glazed faience mostly used for larger vases, architectural decoration and tiles. A considerable number of skilled artists were employed to decorate these wares, notably including the Barlow sisters and George Tinworth, whose work is usually signed with their monograms.

Thomas Fell & Co. Ltd.

St. Peter's Pottery, Newcastle-upon-Tyne. 1817–90.
Impressed marks, 1817–30. Between 1830 and 1890, initials or Christian name initial and full surname were impressed or printed in several forms, '& Co.' being added later.

1   2   3   4

A large group of potteries were situated on the rivers Tyne, Wear and Tees, mostly at Newcastle and Sunderland, and their wares had a predominantly nautical flavour, carried out in washed-in black transfer, often with pink lustre ornamentation. This can be seen in the well-known 'Wear Bridge' jugs, bowls and mugs made by Dixon & Co. of Sunderland. Most of these potters, including Fell, marked some of their products with name marks.

Gildea & Walker
Burslem. 1881–5.
The mark first used by predecessors Bates Elliott & Co. c.
1870 but without the words TRADE MARK, and
afterwards, c. 1885–8, within a double circle, by successors
James Gildea. The figure of the potter is to be found in
various forms of the mark.

T. G. Green & Co. Ltd.
Church Gresley, Nr. Burton-on-Trent. c. 1864 onwards.
The printed 'church mark', first registered in 1888 and
used in various forms afterwards. ENGLAND added after
1891.

Hicks, Meigh & Johnson
Shelton. 1822–35.
Printed mark c. 1822–35, but possibly used also by Hicks
& Meigh (1806–22). The three initial letters appear in
various other printed marks.

Specialising in transfer printing under and over the glaze, and particularly
in deep dark blue underglaze.

Hilditch & Son
Lane End. 1822–30.
Various forms of printed marks bearing initials.

Samuel Hollins
Shelton. c. 1784–1813.
Impressed marks, but many pieces are unmarked.

S.HOLLINS

HOLLINS

Noteworthy for his red and chocolate-coloured unglazed stoneware decorated with raised designs in the Elers style, and for green stoneware tea and coffee-pots decorated with applied blue jasper ornament. Many of these designs were copied from silver shapes. The use of lustre bands, particularly around the rims of mugs and tankards, and not unlike gun-metal in appearance, was a speciality of Hollins, one of the early proprietors of the New Hall porcelain works.

Johnson Bros. (Hanley) Ltd.
Hanley, from 1883, and at Tunstall c. 1899–1913.
Most marks, impressed or printed, are of this name mark type, and some incorporate pattern names.

Lowesby Pottery

Leicestershire. c. 1835–40.
1. & 2. Impressed, c. 1835–40.
3. Printed, c. 1835–40.

LOWESBY

1

2

3

Under Sir Francis Fowke, red terra-cotta ware covered with dull black was manufactured, and brightly painted with enamels, this painting possibly not being done in the actual factory.

Leeds Pottery

Hunslet, Leeds, under various proprietors. c. 1758–1880.
1. Impressed, c. 1775–c. 1800. The same words in lower case letters on printed cream-ware c. 1790 onwards.
2. & 3. Impressed, c. 1781–1820.

LEEDS POTTERY

1

HARTLEY, GREENS & CO.

2

HARTLEY GREENS & CO
LEEDS POTTERY

3

Although ordinary earthenwares and black basalts were made by the various proprietors, the fame of Leeds rests upon its fine cream-ware, much of which is unmarked. At first imitative of Wedgwood ware and intending to rival porcelain in lightness, durability and cheapness, the best Leeds cream-ware often surpasses Wedgwood in its design and technical excellence. Much is finely pierced and so greatly admired by collectors, that it is often forged. But modern copies lack the fine potting, are heavier in weight, and have a thick, white, glassy glaze unlike that of true Leeds, which has a greenish tint in the crevices.

Martin Brothers

Fulham and Southall, London. 1873–1914. The brothers were Robert Wallace, Walter, Edwin and Charles.

1. Incised, 1873–4. C3 refers to the model.
2. Incised, 1874–78. Note that the letter before the numeral is discontinued.
3. Incised, c. 1878–9.
4. Incised, c. 1879–82.

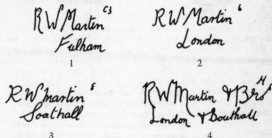

All four brothers had formal artistic training, and Walter and Edwin had been employed at Doultons. Although their productions of salt-glazed stoneware included everyday vases, bottles, bowls, jugs, etc. in the Doulton style, their fame rests most upon their grotesque, sometimes almost ugly caricatures of human faces, birds and beasts in the shape of jugs and other suitable forms.

Charles James Mason & Co.

Patent Ironstone China Manufactory, Lane Delph. 1829–45. Previously G. M. and C. J. Mason, and subsequently C. J. Mason.

1. & 2. Versions of the standard Ironstone mark used by G. M. and C. J. Mason 1813–29, and subsequently throughout the life of the factory, being used after 1862 by Ashworths who later added their own name. The word IMPROVED occurs c. 1840.

(contd.)

3. A version of the basic mark, but without the scroll, c. 1845.
4. Printed mark c. 1825, with pattern numbers beneath. There are several other printed marks of the period 1829–45 using the same words.

3   4

'Mason's Patent Ironstone China' was introduced in an attempt to provide the industrial middle-class with a cheap, durable, colourful substitute for the splendid Chinese porcelain owned by the wealthy. Articles included enormous vases, some of them replicas of the Oriental, fireplace surrounds, bed-posts, large dinner-services and, of course, many sizes of the typical octagonal jug with snake or dragon handle. Much of the decoration was transferred and washed in with enamels, and the sometimes garish blues, reds and greens enriched with gilding of good quality. Occasionally one finds better pieces bearing panels of well-painted landscape or flowers. A class of ware which is seldom marked is completely covered with a deep blue enamel (which usually trespasses a little upon the white base of the article), upon which decoration is applied in gold, sometimes tooled, in bright enamels, or in a combination of both.

Elijah Mayer
Cobden Works, Hanley. c. 1790–1804. Succeeded by Elijah Mayer & Son, 1805–34.
1. Impressed, c. 1790–1804.
2. Impressed or printed, 1805–34.

E.MAYER   'E. Mayer & Son'
1   2

Middlesborough Pottery Co.
Middlesborough-on-Tees. 1834–44.
An example of the anchor mark, found either with initials or with the name in full, which in turn may be found without the anchor.

Minton
Stoke, under various names. 1793 onwards.
1. Moulded, on moulded wares c. 1830–40.
2. Printed, c. 1900–8.

1

2

Thomas Minton (1765–1836) was formerly an engraver at Spodes, after serving an apprenticeship at Caughley under Thomas Turner, for whom he engraved several underglaze-blue designs, including the well-known 'Broseley Dragon'. 'Stone China' was made at Mintons, very similar to that introduced by Mason, decorated mainly in Oriental style, as in the case of the famous 'Amherst Japan' pattern made in honour of Lord Amherst, Governor General of India.

Bernard Moore
Wolfe Street, Stoke. 1905–15.
1. Painted mark found in various forms, 1905–15.
2. Painted or printed, sometimes with the year, 1905–15.

Bernard Moore's factory should not be confused with that of the Moore Brothers (1782–1905) who preceded him, and whose wares bear self-explanatory impressed or printed marks.

BM

1

BERNARD **M**OORE

2

Few potters have imitated so successfully the Chinese 'sang-de'boeuf', plain or flambé, sometimes bearing designs in blue, black, turquoise, gold and other bright colours. Moore was able to produce a wide range of splashed or transmutation glazes, including a fine 'peach-bloom', often as brilliant as the true Chinese.

Myatt Pottery Co.

Bilston, Staffs.

The impressed mark, registered in 1880 and used until c. 1894.

MYATT

Not to be confused with the name mark used by other potters of the same name working in the Potteries during the late 18th and 19th centuries.

James Neale & Co.

Church Works, Hanley. c. 1776–c. 1786. Subsequently Messrs. Neale & Wilson and, in 1795, Robert Wilson.

1. Impressed mark of James Neale & Co., c. 1776–86. Impressed initials and names also used.
2. Impressed, with crescent or G, used by Neale & Co., c. 1780–90.
3. Impressed, c. 1784–95.
4. Impressed, c. 1795–1800.

1

2

NEALE & WILSON

3

WILSON

4

Makers of fine figures, usually in the classical style, since the famous French modeller Voyez worked at the factory. In addition, stoneware jugs with cupids in relief, baskets and, rather later, after Wilson joined the firm, an improved cream-ware, silver lustre and pink lustre in the Wedgwood style.

Pearson & Co.

Chesterfield. Est. 1805.

Impressed and printed, c. 1880. Before this date impressed marks P&CO or the name in full.

Benjamin Plant
Lane End, Longton. c. 1780–1820.
Incised mark c. 1780–1820. Many other potters of the
same name worked in Staffordshire towards the end of the
19th century, for the most part using name marks.

B Plant
Lane End.

Portobello
Near Edinburgh. c. 1764 onwards.
Mark of Thomas Rathbone & Co., from 1810 onwards.
Other Portobello potters were Scott Brothers 1786–96 and
A. W. Buchan & Co. Ltd., from 1867 onwards, whose
marks are self-explanatory.

F. & R. Pratt & Co. Ltd.
*Fenton. Est. c. 1818. Taken over by the Cauldron Potteries
Ltd. in the 1920's. Formerly Felix Pratt.*
1. Printed, c. 1818–60. Other marks are initials, and
initials with '& Co' added c. 1840.
2. & 3. Printed, on coloured transfer-printed wars of the
'Pot Lid' type, sometimes with pattern numbers.

PRATT   PRATT   F&R PRATT &
                FENTON   268
                               FENTON
1   2   3

Above all, a company noted for the production of underglaze printed lids of
pomade-pots called 'Pot Lids', and of dessert services andother domestic
wares upon which the same pot-lid prints were often used. Many engravers
such as the William Brooke mentioned by Simeon Shaw and Austin of
Pratts, did much to develop the new process, in which every colour was
printed separately, each being allowed to dry for a day or so, in contrast to
the quicker and cheaper lithographic process.

Rockingham Works

Swinton, Yorkshire. c. 1745–1842.

1. An impressed mark of John and William Brameld, c. 1778–1842. Many other impressed marks, some including the word ROCKINGHAM.
2. Impressed, c. 1806 onwards.
3. Relief mark, c. 1806 onwards.

BRAMELD

1

ROCKINGHAM

2

3

Best known of the earthenware made at Swinton is the brown-glazed cream-ware used extensively between about 1796 and 1806, and usually called 'Rockingham Ware', though in fact it was made also at other Staffordshire potteries. Among typical pieces are many kinds of brandy flasks in the shapes, for example, of shoes, pistols, etc., Toby jugs, and the famous peach-shaped 'Cadogan' tea-pot.

Royal Essex Pottery

Also known as Hedingham Art Pottery. Castle Hedingham, Essex. 1864–1901.

Applied mark in relief used 1864–1901 on so-called 'Castle Hedingham' wares, and often removed in fraudulent attempts to pass them off as much earlier pieces. An incised mark including the proprietor's name is also found.

Ralph Salt
Marsh Street, Hanley. c. 1820–46.
Impressed on scroll in relief on the backs of bases of figures.

Salt was born in 1782 and died in 1846, and was one of the most notable figure-makers in the Walton style, his models being similar in design and in colouring, though he occasionally used metallic lustre either by itself or with enamels. A feature of some of his figures is the title impressed on the front of the base.

Scott Brothers
Portobello, Nr. Edinburgh. c. 1786–96.
An example of the various impressed name marks.

SCOTT BROS

Shorthose & Heath
Hanley. c. 1795–1815.
Impressed or printed c. 1795–1815.

**SHORTHOSE &
HEATH**

Shorthose & Co.
Hanley. Successors to Shorthose & Heath. c. 1817–1822.
Printed in blue on blue-printed wares. The name mark without the crescents is also found, in upper case letters, in impressed, printed and painted forms.

Shorthose & Co
CC

Notably makers of white earthenware printed overglaze in red, of rustic subjects such as 'Children at Play' and of cream-ware including plates and dishes with embossed wicker-work pierced rims.

Spodes

Stoke-on-Trent. Various titles – Josiah Spode c. 1784–1833, Copeland & Garrett 1833–47, W. T. Copeland & Sons Ltd., 1847 to present day.

1. & 2. Impressed on blue-printed wares, c. 1784–1800.
3. Impressed on the 'New Stone' body, c. 1805–20.
4. Printed in black c. 1805–15, inblue c. 1815–30.
5–7. Printed, c. 1805–33.
8. Printed, 1867–90.

Among the many achievements of this great pottery were great advances made in the process of transfer printing, not only in underglaze blue, but also in colour, particularly when applied to the durable stone chinas. Much use was made of printed outline which was then filled in with enamels in many different colour schemes to give wide ranges of cheaply produced patterns.

Andrew Stevenson

Cobridge. c. 1816–30.

1. Impressed, c. 1816–30, and also found with initial.
2. Impressed, c. 1820.
3. Impressed, c. 1816–30.

STEVENSON

1   2   3

Ralph Stevenson
Cobridge. c. 1810–32.
One of numerous impressed marks. Sometimes the initial
only, and sometimes with '& Son'.

R. STEVENSON

Stevenson & Williams
*Cobridge. c. 1825. According to Godden, a partnership
between Ralph Stevenson and Aldborough Lloyd Williams.*
1. Printed mark.
2. Printed mark on pieces decorated with American views.

Stubbs & Kent
Longport. c. 1828–30.
Impressed or printed. Also used by Joseph Stubbs of
Longport, who was probably connected in some way with
this firm. His wares usually bear impressed name marks,
and may be dated c. 1822–35.

Swansea
Cambrian Pottery. c. 1783–1870.
1–4. Impressed, c. 1783_c. 1810.
5. Impressed or printed, c. 1811–17, in various forms.
6. Impressed, c. 1824–50.
7. Printed, c. 1862–70, in various forms.

SWANSEA
1

CAMBRIA
2

CAMBRIAN
3

CAMBRIAN POTTERY
4

DILLWYN & CO.
5

DILLWYN
6

D. J. EVANS & CO.
7

It should be noted that for part of this time a rival pottery at Glamorgan (c. 1814–39) made 'opaque china' and cream-ware. Among Cambrian Pottery products were fine black basalt, underglaze blue-painted, blue-printed and black-printed wares, a red earthenware impressed with classical subjects in black called 'Dillwyn's Etruscan Ware' made between 1847 and 1850, and above all, an improved, whiter cream-ware enamelled by W. W. Young, Thomas Pardoe, and other outstanding artists.

W. Howson Taylor
Ruskin Pottery, Smethwick, Birmingham. 1898–1935.
1. Impressed, c. 1898–early 19th century.
2. & 3. Painted or incised of the same period. Latrer marks are self-explanatory.

TAYLOR
1

2

3

Howson Taylor's 'Ruskin' pottery was an attempt to rival Chinese coloured glazes in every colour from white to sang-de-boeuf, often with fine flambé effects.

Charles Tittensor
Shelton. c. 1815–23. Various partnerships.
Printed on printed wares, and impressed on very rare figures.

TITTENSOR

Maker of figures with bocage or tree backgrounds which may be looked upon as transitional between the Wood coloured glaze ones and the enamelled variety of Walton and Salt. The few authentic specimens known are rather crudely modelled and enamelled in attractive blue, green, yellow and orange-yellow.

John Turner
Lane End, Longton. c. 1762–1806. Not to be confused with Thomas Turner of Caughley.
1. Impressed mark from c. 1770 onwards, usually on stonewares.
2. Printed or impressed from 1784, sometimes with the name beneath.

1

2

One of Wedgwood's rivals in the making of fine jasper wares in the classical style, and a maker of fine stoneware of warm biscuit tint, sharply modelled in relief, and often enhanced with bands of blue or brown enamel. His black basalts are equal to those of Wedgwood and he is said to have been a pioneer of underglaze-blue printing in the Potteries.

John Voyez
Staffordshire modeller to Ralph and other members of the Wood family. c. 1768–1800.
An example of the various impressed name marks, on such modelled specimens as the 'Fair Hebe' jug.

J. VOYEZ

A typical example of the nomadic craftsman who worked for many potters, including Wedgwood and Neale & Co.

John Walton
Burslem. c. 1818–35.
Impressed mark on a relief scroll on the backs of bocage figures.

Probably the most important potter to follow the figure-making tradition of the Woods, making gay, colourful and attractive figures with bocage backgrounds in emulation of Chelsea and Derby porcelain. His pieces were intended to be the poor man's porcelain, and were designed to stand against the wall and so to be viewed only from the front. His range of subjects was wide – religious, historical, sporting, and rustic, and he often assembled a series of stock motifs, such as cows, dogs, sheep or human figures into different composite models.

John Warburton
Cobridge. c. 1802–25.
Impressed. The name is also found but usually with the addition of initials and/or place names, on wares made by others of the same name, e.g. John Warburton of Gateshead c. 1750–95, Peter Warburton of Cobridge c. 1802–12, and Peter and Francis Warburton of Cobridge c. 1795–1802.

WARBURTON

Watson's Pottery
Prestonpans, Scotland. c. 1750–1840.
Impressed, c. 1770–1800. Self-explanatory marks thereafter.

WATSON

Josiah Wedgwood & Sons Ltd.
Burslem. c. 1759, Etruria c. 1769, Barlaston 1940.
1–3. Impressed marks. 1 and 3 c. 1759–69, and 2 the standard mark c. 1759 onwards. From 1860 a three-letter dating system was used and from 1891 'ENGLAND' was added. 'MADE IN ENGLAND' signifies a 20th century origin.

(contd.)

Wedgwood   WEDGWOOD   WEDGWOOD

1   2   3

4. Impressed on ornamental wares of the Wedgwood and Bentley period, c. 1768–80.

WEDGWOOD
& BENTLEY

4

5. Impressed on small cameos, plaques, etc., Wedgwood and Bentley period, c. 1768–80.

W & B

5

6. Impressed or in relief on vases etc. of the Wedgwood and Bentley period, c. 1768–80.

6

7. Modern mark, impressed, c. 1929 onwards.

WEDGWOOD

7

8. & 9. Misleading marks of Wedgwood & Co. Ltd., Unicorn and Pinnox Works, Tunstall, c. 1860 onwards, and John Wedge Wood of Burslem and Tunstall, c. 1845–60.

WEDGWOOD & CO.

8

J. WEDGWOOD

9

Apart from his fame a a developer of the classical spirit in his wonderful jasper ware, Wedgwood also brought cream-ware to a high standard of excellence for domestic use. He also invented or improved variegated wares which imitated marble and other natural stones, the red ware called 'rosso antico' which was sometimes decorated with bright enamels, and the well-known, clean-looking 'cauliflower' wares.

Enoch Wood
Burslem. c. 1784–1790.
1–3. Examples of the various name marks on domestic wares, figures, plaques, etc. Though a modeller of note, he did not set up a factory of his own until 1784.

ENOCH WOOD
SCULPSET

E WOOD

Enoch Wood &Co

1   2   3

Known in his day as the 'Father of the Potteries', and a capable potter and modeller beside being one of the first recorded students and actual collectors of early pottery. He is best known for his portrait busts in black basalt, black-enamelled cream-ware and painted cream-ware, and his vast output also included blue-printed earthenwares bearing landscapes and figure subjects intended for the American market.

Wood & Caldwell
Burslem. c. 1790–1818. Successors to Enoch Wood.
Impressed mark.

WOOD & CALDWELL

Enoch Wood & Sons
Burslem. 181–46. Successors to Wood & Caldwell.
Impressed. Other self-explanatory name marks also used.

Other Marks

Registration Marks
1842–1883

A diamond-shaped mark, printed or impressed, is often seen on wares first made between 1842 and 1883, indicating that to prevent piracy a particular design of an article had been registered with the London Patent Office. It will of course be clear that the information thus given in the marks will only indicate the earliest possible date of manufacture, since the design so registered could have been used in succeeding years.

Year Letters in top angle of diamond
1842–67

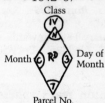

A 1845	G 1863	M 1859	S 1849	Y 1853
B 1858	H 1843	N 1864	T 1867	Z 1860
C 1844	I 1846	O 1862	U 1848	
D 1852	J 1854	P 1851	V 1850	
E 1855	K 1857	Q 1866	W 1865	
F 1847	L 1856	R 1861	X 1842	

Year Letters in right-hand angle of diamond
1868–83

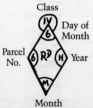

193

A	1871	H	1869	P	1877	X	1868
C	1870	I	1872	S	1875	Y	1879
D	1878	J	1880	U	1874		
E	1881	K	1883	V	1876		
F	1873	L	1882	W	1878		

Month Letters – the same for both arrangements

A – December	H – April
B – October	I – July
C or O – January	K – November and December 1860
D – September	M – June
E – May	R – August, and Sept. 1–19, 1857
G – February	W – March

Registration Numbers
from 1884

Numbers prefixed 'Rd.' or 'Rd. No.' are found on many wares made from January 1884 onwards, of which a full list may be found in G. A. Godden's 'Encyclopaedia' of marks, pages 527–8.

Minton Year Cyphers

Much Minton ware may be identified and dated by the presence thereon of impressed year cyphers which were introduced in 1842.

1842	1843	1844	1845	1846
✳	△	◻	✕	⬭

1847	1848	1849	1850	1851
⌒	⊶	✕	♧	∴

1852	1853	1854	1855	1856
V	⊛	ˮ	✳	φ

1857	1858	1859	1860	1861
◇	ᵾ	✗	℧	人

1862	1863	1864	1865	1866
♄	⊖	Z	✾	✗

Minton Year Cyphers

1867	1868	1869	1870	1871
⚹	匚	⊡	ⓜ	ℵ

1872	1873	1874	1875	1876
⊗	⚹	↓	ℰ	⬙

1877	1878	1879	1880	1881
⬭	△	⬘	⧊	⊞

1882	1883	1884	1885	1886
⊗	◑	⊠	⋈	B

1887	1888	1889	1890	1891
♔	♉	S	T	♍

1892	1893	1894	1895	1896
♉	♉	♉	⬡	⬡

1897	1898	1899	1900	1901
⬡	⬡	⬡	⬡	①

1902	1903	1904	1905	1906
②	③	④	⑤	⑥

1907	1908	1909	1910	1911
⑦	⑧	♑	♋	⬙

1912	1913	1914	1915	1916
♌	⚒	☆	✿	⚜

1917	1918	1919	1920	1921
✵	✹	⚲	⚶	⚜

195

Minton Year Cyphers

1922	1923	1924	1925	1926
ᴨᴍ	╫	✿	☆	⋏
1927	1928	1929	1930	1931
⅏	⬡	⋈	⚒	⚑
1932	1933	1934	1935	1936
⛰	⋀	◆	⚲	∞
1937	1938	1939	1940	1941
⊙	✠	⛵	◗	✦
1942				
⋁				

The Royal Arms Mark

Many printed marks upon 19th and 20th century wares incorporate a version of the Royal Arms, often with self-explanatory names and place-names. In their absence, it is difficult to attribute origin, though the actual form of the Arms themselves provides a clue as to date of manufacture. Thus, before 1837 we find an extra tiny shield in the centre which is missing in later versions.

The Staffordshire Knot Mark

Many firms in the Potteries used the 'Staffordshire Knot' as a mark usually with distinguishing initials in the three loops. H. Aynsley & Co., H.A. & Co., 1873–1932 is a good example of this (see p. 169).

Pilkington's Tile & Pottery Co. Ltd.
Clifton Junction, Nr. Manchester
c. 1897–1938 and 1948–57

Many potters have tried to emulate the lovely coloured glazes of the Orientals, among them William de Morgan, Bernard Moore, W. Howson Taylor (Ruskin Pottery) and William and Joseph Burton of Pilkingtons and the Royal Lancastrian Pottery. At the beginning of the present century the firm was probably the largest manufactory of artistic decorative tiles in the country, specialising in beautiful lustre effects. Since many items were designed by craftsmen of note, we give the marks usually found on examples of their work.

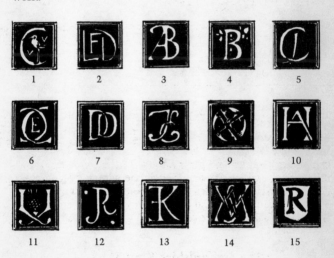

Wedgwood Year Letters
Period 1860–1906

From 1860 onwards earthenwares bear impressed three letter year marks, the last letter denoting the year of manufacture. Thus, O–1860 to Z–1871, A–1872 to Z–1897,
A–1898 to I–1906. This repetition may obviously cause
some confusion, somewhat eased by the appearance of the
word ENGLAND from 1891 onwards. These year marks
are accompanied by the standard impressed WEDGWOOD
factory mark.

Old Sheffield Plate
and Electroplate

Old Sheffield Plate was invented in the middle of the 18th century when it was discovered that a thin layer of silver could be fused onto copper, producing products which looked as if they were made of solid silver but cost a fraction of the price. The designs used by the Sheffield Plate manufacturers were copied from popular styles of silverware, and indeed much Sheffield Plate was made by silversmiths. The success of Sheffield Plate ended in the middle of the 19th century with the discovery of British plate and electroplating.

The marks struck on Old Sheffield Plate are not as helpful as those on silver in helping to establish the date of manufacture, and indeed, from 1773 to 1784 they were actually forbidden in order to prevent Plate being passed off as silver. Nevertheless, there are some guidelines which a collector can follow.

A crown indicates that the item was made between 1765 and 1825.

The words 'Best Sheffield Heavy Silver Plating' were only used after 1820.

Genuine Old Sheffield Plate which has no marks dates from between 1773 and 1784.

Distinguishing Old Sheffield Plate from Electroplate

Electroplaters often tried to make their products look like the more expensive Old Sheffield Plate, but the two can be distinguished by careful inspection.

Old Sheffield Plate has a faint glow which is almost blue. If you come across a more reddish glow, the item is a more thinly silvered foreign import. Electroplated products have a duller appearance.

With any hollow item, the process involved in plating has to leave a seam whereas electroplating does not.

The words 'Sheffield Plated' stamped on an item in fact mean that it is electroplated!

The letters 'BP' denote that the item is British Plate.

The letters 'EP' or 'EPNS' mean that the item is electroplated.

Electroplate

By 1842 Elkington & Co. of Birmingham had perfected the process of silver deposition onto a preformed article. The process became known as electroplating or silver plating.

The article to be plated was placed in a solution of Potassium Cyanide with a negative pole attached to it. The positive pole was attached to a 100 per cent pure silver sheet. A low voltage current was then passed through the solution. This allowed the silver sheet, acting as a cathode, to produce silver ions which passed into the solution and were drawn to the article, acting as an anode, adhering to its surface. The longer the process was operated, the thicker the coating of silver.

The vat containing the solution was lined with Portland cement and had to be kept extremely clean at all times for the process to work, The quality of the finish on the resulting end product depended on this since imperfections could result from the presence of foreign bodies in the solution.

On removal from the vat the article was gently hammered over its surface to make sure that the silver coating had adhered properly. Finally the article was burnished. The most common base metals were Britannia metal and nickel silver. Other base metals used were copper, nickel, brass and British plate.

Old Sheffield Plate production quickly declined with the advent of electroplating and by the 1860s had almost ceased to be manufactured. Some old Sheffield Platers seeking to survive converted over to electroplating and went on to prosper. They produced the majority of electroplated wares and almost without exception, stamped their marks on them. The general rule is that if it is English made and marked, it is probably Sheffield made, and if it is unmarked it is probably Birmingham made. However, beware of teasets

– usually only one article, the tea pot, may be marked.

A lot of modern silver plate purporting to be antique is often sold at high prices in antique shops. Conversely, truly antique pieces often trade at lower prices with the seller and purchaser none the wiser as to the authenticity of the piece. Early pieces of electroplate, often called silver plate, are beautifully crafted and hand engraved and are important historically. If you know what you are looking for, many bargains may be had and good investments made.

Base Metals

COPPER

This was a popular base metal at the start of electroplating. However, as time wore on it was dropped due to its expense. Generally, silver plated copper wares date from the early-mid Victorian period and will often have the letters EP stamped on their bases to denote electroplate. Note, though, copper was still used to a lesser degree in Britain by some firms right up to the twentieth century.

The metal shows through worn areas as a pinkish or sometimes reddish-brown hue.

NICKEL

Pure nickel was first mined in Saxony, Germany c1830. The pure metal was used sparingly throughout the Victorian period but its alloy, nickel silver, was used more extensively since it is a good base metal.

The metal shows through worn areas as a light dull grey colour and wares usually have the letters EP stamped on their bases.

NICKEL SILVER

Also called German silver and in the early days Argentine, it actually contains no silver at all. It is an alloy of copper, zinc and nickel. German silver gets its name from the fact that nickel was first mined at Saxony in Germany.

It was soon discovered by Elkington that this alloy provided a perfect base for electroplating. It was used for this purpose from about 1842 and is still used today.

The yellow/white colour of the base metal allows easy identification on worn areas.

The words 'Hardsoldered' are occasionally seen stamped incuse on the base of the articles. Hard solder was used on electroplated wares prior to plating and is an alloy which contains 50/50 nickel and silver.

Wares will have the letters EPNS or EPGS denoting electroplated nickel silver and electroplated German silver respectively. Various combinations of letters are also used, i.e. EP, NS and GS.

Understandably the name German silver was dropped around the time of the First World War for patriotic reasons.

BRITANNIA METAL

This alloy was developed c1770 as a cheap alternative to Old Sheffield Plate and gained increasing popularity from its inception. Around 1846 it was discovered that Britannia metal could be silver plated.

Electroplating was very appealing to the Britannia metal smiths as the alloy plated very well and since their original plan was to produce a less expensive substitute to Old Sheffield Plate, electroplating was a real bonus for it brought them ever closer to their objective. Nearly all the fifty or so Britannia metal makers of Sheffield had by 1880 converted to electroplating merely by the inclusion of plating vats.

By 1870 labour costs became an increasing burden to the costs of manufactured goods and what with intense competition, it's not surprising that many Britannia metal firms started producing wares of poor quality, thin gauge and only a light coating of silver. It is these cheap electroplated wares produced during the late Victorian period that gave Britannia metal a bad reputation for being a base metal of cheap wares.

The letters EPBM are usually stamped on the base of wares denoting electroplated Britannia metal.

Although this alloy was used from 1846, the abbreviation EPBM didn't come into general use until 1855. In the past goods that were badly worn were discarded as junk. However Britannia metal, being pewter, is collectable in its own right, particularly Victorian wares that are becoming ever more sought after.

BRITISH PLATE

This is a form of nickel silver. The letters BP are marked on goods denoting British Plate.

Design Registration Marks

Some metal wares may be dated approximately if their design was registered. Look out for a diamond shape impressed mark (1843–1883) or an impressed registration number from 1884.

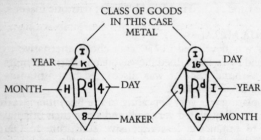

<table>
<tr><th colspan="4">1842–1867</th><th colspan="3">1868–1883</th></tr>
</table>

Year Letter Codes 1842–1867				Year Letter Codes 1868–1883			
A	1845	N	1864	A	1871	V	1876
B	1858	O	1862	C	1870	W	1878
C	1844	P	1851	D	1878	X	1868
D	1852	Q	1866	E	1881	Z	1879
E	1855	R	1861	F	1873		
F	1847	S	1849	H	1869		
G	1863	T	1867	I	1872		
H	1843	U	1848	J	1880		
I	1846	V	1850	K	1883		
J	1854	W	1865	L	1882		
K	1857	X	1842	P	1877		
L	1856	Y	1853	S	1875		
M	1859	Z	1860	U	1874		

The months were the same for both series.

A December (except 1860)	E May	K November and December 1860
B October	G February	M June
C January	H April	O January
D September	I July	R August and 1–19 September 1857
		W March

The day of the month was marked as the numbered date, i.e. the 8th was marked 8.

From 1884 registration numbers took over from the diamond registration mark:

1884	1 – 19753	1895	246975 – 268391
1885	19754 – 40479	1896	268392 – 291240
1886	40480 – 64519	1897	291241 – 311657
1887	64520 – 90482	1898	311658 – 331706
1888	90483 – 116647	1899	331707 – 351201
1889	116648 – 141272	1900–1909	351202 – 551999
1890	141273 – 163766	1910–1919	552000 – 673749
1891	163767 – 185712	1920–1929	673750 – 751159
1892	185713 – 205239	1930–1939	751160 – 837519
1893	205240 – 224719	1940–1949	837520 – 860853
1894	224720 – 246974		

Makers' and other Marks

Most Sheffield platers stamped their initials e.g. James Dixon & Sons stamped their wares JD & S. However some of the Britannia metal smiths involved with electroplating stamped the company name in full or just their surname e.g. Philip Ashberry.

MAKER'S MARK

Knowing who the maker is and their dates of manufacture establishes a lower and upper date of any article, e.g. Joseph Ridge was only in production during 1881–1886 (see mark 572). Knowing when changes occurred to the company title can distinguish earlier pieces from later pieces. For instance, when '& Sons', 'Co.' or new partners were added, e.g. '& Sons' was added to Philip Ashberry in 1856 (see pg. 226).

TRADE MARKS

Many companies had trademarks which could be registered from c1878. E.g. James Dixon & Sons used a trumpet and banner which was put on all their wares from 1879. Therefore pieces not having this trademark are most definitely prior to 1879.

MISLEADING INITIALS

Beware that sometimes an 'I' will replace 'J', e.g. some early James Dixon and John Harrison pieces have been seen with the stamp marks I D & S and I H & Co. respectively.

A1

This is stamped on many wares and is just a sales ploy used to imply quality.

ELECTROPLATED

This word was stamped incuse on many wares during the period 1842–1855 before the abbreviation EPNS and EPBM came into general use.

ENGLAND

Never found on goods before 1890. Commonly found on ware c1890–1920.

MADE IN ENGLAND

Commonly found on wares c1920–present day.

CROWN INSIDE SHIELD

A crown inside a shield denotes the Victorian period prior to 1897. The mark of course mimicked the crown used to assay silver at Sheffield. Its use stopped c1897 after the guardians at the Sheffield Assay office threatened legal action.

PLUMES

Sometimes found on Victorian goods.

INITIALS

The majority of firms stamped their wares with their initials plus an 'S' at the end and in a sequence of four punches to mimic sterling silver. The marks were invariably in intaglio, that is punched in with the letters in relief. Some early marks, particularly with Britannia base metal, were stamped incuse with the company name in full.

SINGLE NUMBER

Usually indicating the capacity in half pints. However it may also denote a variation in size of a particular style or even the workman's number.

OTHER LETTERS

A single or pair of letters may indicate the workman's initials.

Dating from the Styles Used

Knobs	Fruit and vegetable designs	1845–c1890
	Bird and animal designs	1850–c1875
	Bone, ivory and mother of pearl	1870–1880
Feet	Many designs were used throughout the Victorian period some of which are Rim, Ball, Lion Paw, Shell motif, Claw and Horse Foot.	
Spouts	Fluted base	1845–1855
	Embossed leaf design	1855–1875
Body	Fruit and vegetable shapes, e.g. Pear shape were popular c1850–c1860, and heavily embossed bodies c1865–c1880.	

Borders Shell and gadroon borders were popular throughout the Victorian period. Scroll borders became popular from c1850–1895.

Victorian Techniques and Styles

It is worth noting that the style trends listed here were also followed by craftsmen making silver or pewter ware.

1840s	Many electroplated wares were cast in parts and soldered together rather than produced by spinning on a lathe.
1840–1865	Antiquarianism. The Rococo revival came into being. From about 1840–1850 unembossed styles like the melon shaped teapots were popular. From about 1850 complex embossing was employed.
1840–c1880	Organic naturalism was very much in vogue and involved the copying of natural objects.
1849	Pierced articles, e.g. salvers were produced no earlier than this date.
1855–1875	Adams or Louis XVI revival period brought hanging festoons, urns, rams heads, corn husks and paterae.
1855–1875	Etruscan or Graeco roman antiquities came into fashion.
1865–1910	Neo classical style came into vogue, the Adams style flowing into it with typical cast bead borders with swags, paterae and scrolling foliage. Flat chased and engraved decorations were used. Fern leaf and flower designs were very popular during this period.
1865–1890s	Japanese style.
1870–1885	Indian style.
1870–1895	Egyptian style. Ethnic styles were very popular from mid-late Victorian period.
1880s–c1910	Arts and crafts movement incorporating plain traditional designs not usually

decorated, the period was also known as Art Nouveau. The hand beaten appearance of planished articles was popular during this period. There are many books on the market that will explain these styles in a lot more detail.

What to Collect

If you want to collect by company name undoubtedly the firm at the top of the list is James Dixon & Sons. Their reputation is unsurpassed by any of the other Sheffield platers. Their wares are still relatively plentiful and are thus fairly easy to collect at a modest price.

Flatware or cutlery on the other hand is far easier to collect, as huge quantities of it were produced from mid Victorian times. For this reason, masses of it turns up everywhere for as little as five pence an item. Forget forks as they are generally not collectable, but spoons on the other hand have a devout following. Antique spoons, particularly seventeenth and eighteenth century, are very rare, expensive and are beyond the means of modest collectors who have turned their attention to nineteenth century spoons thus including electroplated spoons in their collections.

Caution must be exercised as a lot of it is junk – avoid damaged or worn pieces, or any pieces where the silver coating has worn away. Some of the most collectable types of spoon are the caddie spoon, jam spoon and tea spoon. Spoons in the Art Nouveau style are particularly desirable to the collector of nineteenth century spoons, but are extremely rare to find these days and are usually very expensive.

The Makers' Marks

The marks shown on the following pages are not generally shown to scale but are often enlarged to show clarity of detail. Also, variations may exist because over the years different punches may have been used.

Because the actual marks are often taken from pieces true to life, some of the detail may have been lost due to wear and tear. This can well be excused by the fact that the marks shown are representative of the condition you are most likely to find them in.

The dates given are as accurate as can be and are based on company records and dates extensively researched at the local studies and archives department of Sheffield libraries.

Generally the electroplaters stamped their wares with their initials using upper case letters and the ampersand (&) where necessary, in a series of four punch marks. Beware there are exceptions and caution must be exercised.

Where there are not enough letters to make up the required number, then often unrelated letters are used and added at the end of the sequence. A very common letter used was 'S'. John Harrison sometimes used the letters 'NW' denoting Norfolk works.

Britannia metal makers sometimes stamped their wares with their full name or surname, address and the word Sheffield prior to plating. Examples of companies that did this are Philip Ashberry & Sons and John Harrison.

Different companies with the same surname may or may not be related. Connections can sometimes only be inferred by date sequencing.

Introduction to the Tables

The marks illustrated in the following Tables have been treated in two sections. The first contains all the marks containing initials. Where the mark contains a name, the mark is listed under the initial letter of the surname. Where the mark only contains initials it is listed under the first initial, reading from left to right, unless another of the initials is clearly dominant. The second section contains pictorial marks. Makers marked OSP are Old Sheffield Plate makers. Other marks are for electroplated wares.

A

Ashford Ellis & Co.	OSP 1770	
A. Hatfield	OSP1808	
Atkin	From 1853	
Atkin	20th Century	
J. Allgood	OSP 1812	
G. Ashforth & Co.	OSP 1784	
Ashley	OSP 1816	
Askew	OSP 1828	A SKEW MAKER NOTTINGHAM
E. Allport	OSP 1812	

B

Boulton & Fothergill	OSP 1764	
Briddon	1863–1910	
Briddon	1863–1910	
Briddon	1863–1910	
W. Banister	OSP 1808	

G. Beldon	OSP 1809	
Beldon, Hoyland & Co.	OSP 1785	
H. Best	OSP 1814	
Best & Wastidge	OSP 1816	
W. Bingley	OSP 1787	
Thomas Bishop	OSP 1830	
J. Bradshaw	OSP 1822	
Brittain, Wilkinson & Brownhill	OSP 1785	
Brittain, Wilkinson & Brownhill	OSP 1785	
Brumby	1889–1897	

C

J. Gilbert	OSP 1812	
J. Gilbert	OSP 1812	
J. Gilbert	OSP 1812	
Cooper	1867–1964	

Creswick	1863–1890	
Hawksworth	1867–1869	SIBERIAN SILVER
Roberts	1879–1892	
Sissons	1885–1891	
T. Cheston	OSP 1809	
T. Child	OSP 1812	
W. Coldswell	OSP 1806	
C. G. Cope	OSP	
J. Corn and J. Sheppard	OSP 1819	
J. Cracknall	OSP 1814	
T. & J. Creswick	OSP 1811	
J. F. Causer	OSP 1824	
Land	1920–1944	TRADE CIVIC MARK E. P. B. M.
Land	1945–1977	REGISTERED CIVIC TRADEMARK 8194 E. P. B. M. MADE IN ENGLAND

D

D. Not attributed	OSP 1760	
J. Dixon & Sons	OSP 1835	
J. Dixon & Sons	OSP 1835	
J. Davis	OSP 1816	
Deakin Smith & Co.	OSP 1785	
J. Dixon & Sons	OSP 1835	
J. Dixon & Sons	OSP 1835	
J. Dixon & Sons	OSP 1835	
T. Dixon & Co.	OSP 1784	
I. Drabble & Co.	OSP 1805	
G. B. Dunn	OSP 1810	
Dixon	1890–c1935	
Fenton	1897–c1910	

E

Roberts	1916–1919	Ⓔ Ⓟ R&D S.L Ⓝ Ⓢ
Roberts	1857–1934	Ⓔ Ⓢ & Ⓢ
W. Ellerby	OSP 1803	ELL ER BY ✖
S. Evans	OSP 1816	S·EVANS

F

Cobb	1905–c1911	F C & Cᵒ S
Fenton	1859–1896	F.Bʀˢ
Fenton	1883–1888	F F S F
Howard	1870–1974	Ⓕ Ⓗ ⬚ Ⓢ 1680
T. Fox & Co.	OSP 1784	FOX PROCTOR ♥ PASMORE & Cᵒ ✚
H. Freeth	OSP 1816	FREETH △
H. Freeth	OSP 1816	Cᴴ K ⊙ ◁ HF
Frogatt, Coldwell & Lean	OSP 1797	FROGATT COLDWELL & LEAN

G

R. Gainsford	OSP 1808	GA
G. Harrison	OSP 1823	GH
G. Harrison	OSP 1823	GH F
G. Gibbs	OSP 1808	GBBS
Bishop	1894–1940	GB &S
Lee	1888–1967	G. L & Cº S SHEFFIELD ELECTROPLATE E. P. B. M
Wish	1878–1934	GW S EPBM 10301
W. Garnett	OSP 1803	GARNETT
Goodman, Gainsforth and Fairbairn	OSP 1800	A GOODMAN & Cº
E. Goodwin	OSP 1795	E GOODWIN
J. Green & Co.	OSP 1799	I·GREEN&Cº
J. Green	OSP 1807	GREEN
W. Green & Co.	OSP 1784	W GREEN &Cº
Graves	1900–1914	J. G. GRAVES EPNS S

H

D. & G. Holly	OSP 1821	
Henry Atkin	OSP 1823	
Henry Hall	OSP 1829	
Tudor & Leader	OSP 1760	$\mathcal{H}\ T\&\mathcal{C}^o$
Tudor & Leader	OSP 1760	
W. Hutton	OSP 1839	
Atkin	From 1853	
Atkin	From 1890	5305
Boardman	1861–1927	H.P 776 5
Fisher	1900–1920	
Hammond	1886–1935	H C & Co S 5 8 5 6

Harrison	1862–1897	
Harrison	1862–1909	
Hawksworth	1853–1867	
Hawksworth	1892–1894	
Walker	1868–1916	
Wilkinson	1843–1871	
Wilkinson	1872–1894	
Wilkinson	1872–1894	
W. Hall	OSP 1820	
W. Hall	OSP 1820	
Joseph Hancock	OSP 1755	
M. Hanson	OSP 1810	
J. Harrison	OSP 1809	
T. Harwood	OSP 1816	
D. Hill & Co.	OSP 1806	

J. Hinks	OSP 1812	
J. Hipkiss	OSP 1808	
J. Hobday	OSP 1829	
H. Holland & Co.	OSP 1784	
Dan Holly, Wilkinson & Co.	OSP 1784	
Dan Holly, Parker & Co.	OSP 1804	
D. & G. Holly	OSP 1821	
D. Horton	OSP 1808	
J. Horton	OSP 1809	
S. & T. Howard	OSP 1809	
W. Hutton	OSP 1807	
W. Hutton	OSP 1831	
W. Hutton	OSP 1837	
Joseph Hancock	OSP 1755	
G. Lees	OSP 1811	
Harrison	1843–1865	HARRISON NORFOLK WORKS SHEFFIELD 2746
Hibbert	1900–1909	S. HIBBERT & SON / YUKON SILVER

I

I. & I. Waterhouse	OSP 1833	
John Littlewood	OSP 1772	IL PLATED
J. Rowbotham & Co.	OSP 1768	IR
John Winter & Co.	OSP 1765	IW
Creswick	1858–1863	I.F.P C & C°
Harrison	1866–1891	I H & Co
Hawksworth	1867–1911	I.H.T SIBERIAN SILVER

J

John Hoyland & Co.	OSP 1764	J H H C
J. Rodgers & Sons	OSP 1822	J R † G R
J. Rodgers & Sons	OSP 1822	JR P † * S
J. Smallwood	OSP 1823	J J
Roberts, Jacob & Samuel	OSP 1765	JSR
John Hoyland	OSP 1764	
Joseph Wilmore	OSP 1807	J W

Bradbury	1863–1867	JB E.B
Bradbury	1889–1892	J.B.
Clarke	1894–1923	J.C & SONS
Creswick	1853–1855	J C N C
Deakin	1871–1898	4 JD A S M 2052
Dixon	1848–1878	JSD
Fenton	1868–1875	J F F & F F
Fenton	1875–1883	J F F F F
Harrison	1843–1865	J H N W 691
Hawksworth	1873–1892	J K B T H G W
Hawksworth	1873–1892	J·K·B
Pinder	1877–1894	J.P. &C°

Potter	1884–1890	
Potter	1884–1921	J. H. P.
Potter	1922–1940	J H P & S
Round	1863–1897	
Townroe	1887–1916	
Turton	1898–1909	0 5 5 0
Turton	1898–1923	
Turton	1910–1923	2 0 4 6
J. Johnson	OSP 1812	
Jones	OSP 1824	
T. Jordan	OSP	

K

S. Kirkby	OSP 1812	

L

Levesley	c1875–1935	
Levesley	c1875–1935	

J. Law & Son	OSP 1807	LAW⌣SON⌒
R. Law	OSP 1807	R.LAW.
Thomas Law	OSP 1758	TᴴᵒLAW
Thomas Law	OSP 1758	LAW
Thomas Law	OSP 1758	THOꞏLAW & Cᵒ
A. C. Lea	OSP 1808	AꞏCLEA
G. Lees	OSP 1811	LEES
John Lilly	OSP 1815	LILLY
Joseph Lilly	OSP 1816	JOSᴹLILLY
M. Linwood & Sons	OSP 1808	LIN WOOD
J. Linwood	OSP 1807	IꞏLIN WOOD IꞏLIN WOOD
J. Linwood	OSP 1807	IꞏLIN WOOD IꞏLIN WOOD
W. Linwood	OSP 1807	IꞏLIN WOOD IꞏLIN WOOD
J. Love & Co. and Love, Silverside, Darby & Co.	OSP 1785	ILOVE & Cᵒ

M

| Richard Morton | OSP 1765 | MᴳSMᴳS |
| Richard Morton | OSP 1765 | MᴳMᴳMᴳ |

Mappin	From 1873	CORPORATE MARK. **M** **TRUSTWORTHY**
Mappin	From 1900	**M** **TRUSTWORTHY**
Mappin	1861–1890	
Martin	1854–1897	
Willis	1872–1885	
F. Maddin & Co.	OSP 1788	F.MADIN&C? ◇
Mappin Brothers	OSP 1850	MAP PIN BROT HERS
W. Markland	OSP 1818	W·MARKLAND
H. Meredith	OSP 1807	MERE DITH
J. Moore	OSP 1784	MOORE
J. Moore	OSP 1784	Moore
F. Moore	OSP 1820	F·MOORE
R. Morton & Co.	OSP 1785	MORTON&CO.
Fisher	1900–1925	MADRAS SILVER
Mappin	20th Century	MAPPIN & WEBB London & Sheffield MAPPIN PLATE W 20152 ½ PINT

N

Nathaniel Smith	OSP 1756	N S
C. Needham	OSP 1821	C NEEDHAM MAKER SHEFFIELD
W. Newbould & Son	OSP 1804	W·NEWBOULD & SONS
J. Nicholds	OSP 1808	J·NICHOLDS
Nodder	1863–1904	5 JOHN NODDER & SONS SHEFFIELD 2 3 5 2
Nodder	1897–1904	NODDERS SILVER

O

T. Oldham	OSP 1860	T OLDHAM MAKER NOTTINGHAM
Nodder	1897–1904	OSMIUM SILVER

P

J. Gilbert	OSP 1812	
J. Prime	OSP 1839	
J. Prime	OSP 1839	PS

Ashberry	1861–1890	
Ashberry	1867–1935	
Ashberry	1880–1935	
Pinder	1923–Present	
Pinder	1877–1894	
J. Parsons & Co.	OSP 1784	
Peak	OSP 1807	
Pemberton & Mitchell	OSP 1817	
R. Pearson	OSP 1811	
J. Prime	OSP 1839	
Mappin	From 1887	
Potter	1884–1921	
Potter	20th Century	

R

| Robert & Briggs | OSP 1860 | |
| Roberts Smith & Co. | OSP 1828 | |

Richardson	1873–1924	
Roberts	1864–1867	
Roberts	1864–1867	
Roberts	1892–c1920	
Roberts	1920–1923	
Roberts Cadman & Co.	OSP 1785	
J. S. Roberts	OSP 1786	
J. Rodgers & Sons	OSP 1822	
J. Rogers	OSP 1819	
W. Ryland & Son	OSP 1807	

S

J. Smith & Son	OSP 1828	
J. Prime	OSP 1839	
S. Colmore	OSP 1790	
S. & T. Howard	OSP 1809	

W. Scott	OSP 1807	
Fenton	1888–1891	
Fenton	1891–1896	
Hutton	20th Century	SINGALESE
Nodder	c1890–1904	
Roberts	1867–1879	S R C B
T. Sansom & Sons	OSP 1821	SAN SOM
R. Silk	OSP 1809	
J. Shepherd	OSP 1817	SHEP HARD
T. Small	OSP 1812	SMALL
Smith & Co.	OSP 1784	SMITH&Cᵒ
Smith, Tate, Nicholson and Hoult	OSP 1810	SMITH&Cᵒ
W. Smith	OSP 1812	SM ITH
I. Smith	OSP 1821	SMITH
J. Smith	OSP 1836	JOSEPHUS SMITH

N. Smith & Co.	OSP 1784	
Staniforth, Parkinson & Co.	OSP 1784	
B. Stot	OSP 1811	
Sykes & Co.	OSP 1784	
Potter	1884–1921	SUPERIOR PLATE

T

T. Butts	OSP 1807	
Bradbury	1867–1878	
Bradbury	1858–1863	
Bradbury	1892–1916	
Creswick	1852–1853	
Land	1901–1919	
Turner	1883–1940	
S. Thomas	OSP 1818	
E. Thomason & Dowler	OSP 1807	

E. Thomason & Dowler OSP	1807	
Tonks & Co.	OSP 1824	TONKS
Samuel Tonks	OSP 1807	TONKS □
Tudor, Leader & Nicholson	OSP 1784	TUDOR & Cº
S. Turley	OSP 1816	S.TURLEY
J. Turton	OSP 1820	TUR TON
J. Turton	OSP 1820	TUR TON.
Turner	1916–1940	T.TURNER & Co LTD *Pedigree Plate*
J. Tyndall	OSP 1813	TYN DALL

W

George Waterhouse & Co.	OSP 1842	WATERHOUSE&Cº
W. Briggs	OSP 1823	
W. Hutton	OSP 1849	W H & S
W. Hutton	1843–1900	WH S B P
Harrison	1857–1918	S
Shirtcliffe	1921–1931	WS & S EPNS A1 MADE IN ENGLAND 1985

Sissons	1858–1885	
Walker	1852–1897	
Walker	from 1862	W & H
Watson	1897–1940	W & G 945
W. Jervis	OSP 1789	W JER VIS
Waterhouse & Co.	OSP 1807	WATERHOUSE&Cº
Watson, Fenton & Bradbury	OSP 1795	WATSON&Cº
Watson, Pass & Co. (Late J. Watson)	OSP 1811	WATSON PASS &Cº H
W. Watson	OSP 1833	W WATSON MAKER SHEFFIELD
W. Hipwood	OSP 1809	WHIP WOOD
J. White and White & Allgood	OSP 1811	WHITE
Joseph Willmore	OSP 1807	PATENT WILLMORES&WILKES
W. Woodward	OSP 1814	WOOD WARD X WOOD WARD X
S. Worton	OSP 1821	S WORTON
J. Wright & G. Fairbairn	OSP 1809	WRIGHT & FAIRBAIRN

S. & C. Young & Co.	OSP 1813	

Pictorial Marks

M. Boulton & Co.	OSP 1784	✿ ✿
Not attributed	OSP 1760	🐛 🐛 🐛
Tudor & Leader	OSP 1760	🦅 🦅 🦅
Fenton Mathews & Co.	OSP 1760	🦅 🦅 🦅 🦅
Not attributed	OSP 1760	🔔 🔔 🔔
John Watson & Son	OSP 1830	✋
Padley Parkin & Co.	OSP 1849	✋
Waterhouse Hatfield & Co.	OSP 1886	🦅
R. Sutcliffe & Co.	OSP 1786	👁
W. Silkirk	OSP 1807	Sel-?
H. Wilkinson & Co.	OSP 1836	🛡

Walker, Knowles & Co.	OSP 1840	
Blagden, Hodgson	OSP 1821	
Smith, Sissons & Co.	OSP 1848	
Roberts, Smith & Co.	OSP 1828	
Ashberry	1861–1915	
Atkin	From 1890	
Bradbury	1853–1897	
Creswick	1855–1890	
Creswick	1852–1855	
Deakin	1855–1891	
Dixon	1848–1878	
Dixon	1848–1878	

Dixon	1879–c1935
Harrison	1862–1909
Hawksworth	1894–1911
Hutton	From 1900–
Mappin	1865–1905
Martin	1880–1934
Potter	1884–1940
Roberts	1895–c1920
Rodgers	1860–1970

Round	1872–1957	
		ALL THE ROUND
		JR&S LD
		E PNS
Rylands	1876–c1910	R S P C²
		E P N S
		SALEM
Sissons	1858–1891	🔔
Viners	1925–1974	👑
		AL PHA
		Viners
Walker	1861–1890	W & H
Walker	1891–1909	W&H
		WALKER&HALL
		SHEFFIELD
		ENGLAND
Walker	1910–1970	W&H
		WALKER&HALL
		SHEFFIELD
		MADE IN ENGLAND